THE PROBLEM CHILD

ALFRED ADLER

The Problem Child

THE LIFE STYLE OF THE DIFFICULT CHILD
AS ANALYZED IN SPECIFIC CASES.

With an Introduction by

KURT A. ADLER

Capricorn Books • New York

Translated from the French by Guy Daniels

MANUFACTURED IN THE UNITED STATES OF AMERICA

* Contents *

"The Life Style"

The present volume was published in German in 1930, as one of the volumes on *Die Technik der Individualpsychologie* [*Technique of Individual Psychology*], and bore the sub-title *Die Seele des schwererziehbaren Schulkindes*. It comprises Alfred Adler's personal interviews with children, their parents and their teachers, in one of his clinics, together with his analysis of these cases.

Alfred Adler had developed a systematic method for the understanding and treatment of the total personality, "Comparative Psychoanalysis", later called "Individual Psychology", by which name it is known today. (It is also frequently referred to as "Adlerian Psychology".)

The term *Individual* Psychology stems from Adler's stress on the *uniqueness* of the individual and his creation of his own "Life Style", as opposed to Freud's stress on *general* instincts or drives, common to all individuals, and the applicability of *general* symbolisms.

Adler emphasized that his psychology was a psychology of *use,* not of *possession,* that is to say, it is more important to understand what an individual *makes* of his abilities and potentialities, than what abilities and potentialities he may *possess.* Heredity and environment are only the building blocks which an individual uses for constructing his unique way of fitting himself into life as he finds it. This, Adler called the individual's "style of life" or "life style".

According to Adler, the construction of the "life style" is completed by the individual at about the age of four or five. His interpretation of what life is, what he is, what others are and what his relationships to others mean, is pretty nearly fixed by that age, and forms his total attitudes to life in all situations. New experiences are, from that time on, interpreted only from the point of view of *his* life style. This results in a biased selection of perceptions, with the exclusion, or at least depreciation, of all those experiences that do not fit his style of life. All thinking, feeling and acting of an individual support his style of life. Thoughts, feelings and actions that would undermine or contradict his life style are largely rejected.

The measure of mental health is, according to Adler, the amount of *Gemeinschaftsgefühl* or *Social Interest,* that a child develops and integrates into his life style. By "social interest" is meant the feeling for, and cooperation with, people, and the feeling of belonging and participating with others for the common good. All main problems in life—friendship, work, love and marriage—demand a large degree of cooperation and social feeling for their successful fulfillment. Confronted with any of these problems, the individual who does not possess a sufficient amount of social feeling will be emotionally unprepared for these tasks, will fear failure, will shrink away from contact and feel excessively inadequate (inferior). Neuroses, psychoses, and character disorders are only "safeguarding devices" ("defense mechanisms") by which an individual tries, in his unique way, to hide his inadequacy from himself and others, and thus sustain the illusion that he is maintaining at least some modicum of self-esteem. The "safeguarding devices" used by an individual are invariably methods and patterns tried and tested from early childhood on, in one form or another.

Social feelings develop in a child from earliest infancy, through the relationship with the mother. To foster the development of these feelings through a genuine loving relationship is, according to Adler, a mother's most important function. She must subsequently encourage the extension of these feelings toward others. If the mother fails in either of these tasks the child will have a hard time in developing his social feelings.

This does not mean that the mother is always at fault if a child fails to develop adequate social feelings. Many children may derive their faulty life style, with the accompanying feelings of social insufficiency, from the fact that life seems just too difficult for them, whether because of an organic inferiority, a weak constitution, or singular environmental circumstances. Their feelings of inferiority may then be so overwhelming that the resultant insecurity may lead them to become overly self-concerned, and thus prevent their social feelings from evolving at all. In this category Adler mentions, particularly, the ugly children, the clumsy children, the children with organic defects, the rejected children and the excessively pampered children. But even in these cases, Adler said, the development of social feelings is possible, and they can compensate for their handicaps in social ways, if they learn to understand that *use* and not possession is the issue in life.

Adler felt that courage, true courage can be shown only by someone imbued with a considerable amount of "Social Interest".

All the errors that a child is apt to retain from his early gropings for concept formation are to be found in his style of life, his adaptation to life. It can change only if the child (or adult) understands the errors, and has the courage to try new, more social ways. Since it is much easier to effect a change in the life style when it has not been long fixed, Adler proposed early treatment of children, and started an extensive program of child guidance in Vienna. By 1927 there were already 22 such clinics in Vienna, all staffed by his pupils. Their number grew to over thirty clinics by 1934, and were the model for much of the child guidance movement all over the world. All the clinics were closed by the fascist dictatorship under Dollfuss, but after the war, some of them resumed their function.

The treatment sessions in these child guidance clinics were held, to a large extent, in public. Psychologists, teachers and interested parents were allowed to sit in, and even to participate in the consultations. Adler felt that this was important to the child, in order to impress upon him that his behavior was of public concern, and was not merely his *private* affair. In addition, of course, it was a great learning experience for child-psychiatrists, psychologists, social workers, teachers and parents.

This volume is presented here for the first time in the English language.

KURT A. ADLER, PH.D., M.D.

September 1962, New York

* Foreword *

"The child is father to the man."

In Individual Psychology this maxim applies to the fullest extent. The first four or five years of a child's life suffice for him to complete his essentially arbitrary training with regard to his impressions. These impressions derive from his physical state as well as from external stimuli. Thereafter the child begins to assimilate and utilize his experiences no longer arbitrarily—and certainly not in accordance with any alleged laws of causality but in terms of his own established style of life and the laws that govern it. The individual, therefore, is determined by his style of life. Its laws govern his feelings, emotions, thoughts and actions for the rest of his life. The creative style of life begins its work. Rules, principles, character traits, and a conception of the world are elaborated in order to facilitate this. A very definite scheme of initiated apperception is established; and the child's actions and conclusions are initiated in complete accordance with the ideal final form toward which he is striving. The child retains in his consciousness whatever proves to be undisturbing and compatible. The rest is forgotten, reduced or continues as an unconscious pattern further removed from criticism or understanding than are the other perceptions. The final impact of this pattern—whether this pattern reinforces conscious dynamic trends, prevents them or paralyzes them by a counter reaction leading to inhibiting conflicts—is always determined in advance by the style of life.

The patterns of the style of life (for instance, the guiding lines of character traits) are built up over a long period of training, for which there can be found both in the conscious and the subconscious, vestiges of memories, yet the driving factors are not supplied by experiences but by the style of life which has formed and directed them, and used them for its own purpose. An adequate understanding makes it possible to grasp the complete accord between the active force of the conscious and that of the unconscious. But the understanding of both the conscious and unconscious is valid only insofar as it is in accord with the sphere of action of the style of life.

When dealing with only a few fragments of the life of the child one may count on a certain degree of probability acquired by long experience which, however limited, enables one to draw certain conclusions. But one must always check very carefully to see whether these conclusions also correspond to the *complete system* of an individual's psychic life. This procedure corresponds perfectly to the requirements of medical diagnosis, another area where we must draw conclusions from a partial symptom, and to limit the sphere of the assumed illness until a second and a third symptom helps us in establishing a precise diagnosis.

In the present work I have tried, while following the description of the "technique of Individual Psychology," to develop from a slightly different point of view, the style of life of *problem children*.

This requires a most intimate knowledge of the technique of Individual Psychology and of its tested resources, as well as the art of correct interpretation.

Here, as in medical diagnosis, one cannot afford to neglect the conjecturing art of correct guessing. This can be justified only by proving that all of the partial symptoms are clearly in accord with the overall picture, and that they show identical dynamisms. Among these strivings, identical in all of their details these are the most important:

1) The degree of cooperation (of the social feeling and of social interest).
2) The characteristic made in which the individual strives for superiority (security, power, perfection, depreciation of others).

These invariable forms of expression may differ in their means but not in their end goals. (The finalism of Individual Psychology.) The degree of courage or of common sense that is manifested, the individual manner of looking at the world, and the usefulness or harmfulness to the community, all reflect the degree of adaptability to social living. The delays in successfully solving the three basic problems of life (community, occupation, love), or the degree of faulty preparation for them reveals the ever-present inferiority complex and its faulty compensation, the superiority complex.

A person who does not recognize, or who has not understood, the existence of a unity within the style of life will never understand the development of faulty personality traits. But whoever has grasped this concept will know that he must treat the style of life, not the symptoms.

I intend to discuss elsewhere the general and special diagnostics of Individual Psychology, and the role and the technique of the counselor.

Dr. Alfred Adler

* Introduction *

Man and his Fellows

It would be very tempting to embellish this theme with beautiful flourishes and an abundance of phrases. Going back to the sources of civilization, I could describe the prodigious effort made toward establishing the unity of humanity, be it within a tribe, a people, a state or a religious community. I could show how this trend has always been represented by some idea of which man was more or less conscious; the unity of humanity from the political or religious point of view.

But I shall not discuss these things. What I would like to do is to show that the strivings toward the creation of unity in human society should not be evaluated only from a moral, political or religious viewpoint, but above all from the viewpoint of scientific truth.

I would like to stress that the life of the human soul is not a "being" but a "becoming". All those who occupy themselves with exhibiting fragments and portions from the life of the soul have not gotten very far, since they believe they are dealing with some sort of machine. As every living organism is striving toward an ideal final form, we find that psychic life is striving to overcome all the difficulties which, on this earth, rise as questions relating to society and the relations between the sexes. The solutions to these problems will not be found in the same way one finds solutions to mathematical problems. I know that they can be solved correctly; but I also know that they can be solved incorrectly.

I would like to inject here, however, that we cannot expect an absolutely correct solution. All we can expect is to try to achieve a goal for each and every individual in such a way that the unity of the human race seems to be safeguarded. What we call "good" is good with respect to its usefulness for all men. Likewise, what we call "beautiful" is only beautiful from such a point of view. Such is the extent to which the notion of community is rooted in language and in ideas. Therefore, we always find in all individual or mass expressions how they relate to the question of the community. No one can break out of this framework. Every movement within this framework already constitutes an answer. Since solutions are found to be correct only if beneficial to the community, we can understand why there is an outburst of resistance within the sphere of human relations when someone responds incorrectly. This always involves the person who is not closely tied to the community, who does not feel himself to be a part of the whole, who does not feel at home within humanity. He should learn to expect not only the advantages offered him by civilization, but also the inconveniences, seeing them as something belonging to him, and accepting them as such. Thus, what we call interest in the community is only one aspect of the close bond with others, what we call courage is the rhythm which an individual has within himself which enables him to feel that he is a part of the whole. We must now be confused when we consider the average of the present development and realize how much there is still lacking. This only provides us with new tasks for our development. We must not look at our existence as something static, as just "being", or a belligerent against the aspiration toward development. We must consider difficulties as problems we have to solve—problems which stimulate us to an active optimism. Only those who were animated by a vigorous optimism had their say in history; they carried forward our development, and they will do so in the future. All others are actually out of place; they hinder the march of progress. They do not experience the exhilarating feeling of those who are aware that they are turning the wheel of progress. The feeling of worth also stems from a close bond with the community of man and from an active participation in the affairs of the time.

These conclusions are derived from observations of Individual Psychology; they are the fruit of long work. To be a man is not merely a figure of speech; it is to be part of the whole—to feel oneself part of the whole. If so many people are still failing to find this path it is due to their own mistakes. Anybody who has grasped the entire context will not hesitate to join the current which is moving toward the good of society.

If we remember how ill-equipped man is in nature, one thing appears to us very plainly: this living being, if left to himself, could certainly not have managed to survive. As far back as we can trace the history of humanity, we can find no evidence of an individual living alone. There has always been the law of the community. This is quite understandable when we realize human feebleness in the face of nature. Man does not have the natural weapons of other living organisms. He does not have the teeth of the carnivores; nor does he have horns, or the speed of the animals. He cannot climb or fly. He does not have the acuteness of vision, hearing or smell which enables other animals to attack and defend themselves, and secure a place on this earth. The health of man's weak organs has always depended upon his joining with others in order to sustain the life of the individual as well as that of the community and this union has given him new strength. When we reflect upon the extent of human culture, we understand that those who created it and used it were not strong enough when faced with the elements of nature; they had to seek our complements and compensations for the things they lacked. Man must learn to conquer nature in order to make use of it. Thus, the joining together was the most important, the greatest, invention of mankind.

In this respect one should not consider mankind alone: in the animal kingdom we also find that the weaker beings assemble in groups to achieve protection or to hunt together. The gorilla, whose strength we admire, and the tiger, the most feared of all animals, have no need of a community. Man, if we imagine him deprived of all the implements of civilization, devoid of all the means his intelligence has devised would be doomed the very first day he found himself alone in a jungle.

Our observation leads even further. Man's most precious acquisitions in the course of evolution have come to him because of his weakness. If we think of the life of man, of the existence of the human race, we cannot comprehend his survival unless we consider the tremendous aid which he has gained by joining in a community. Naturally, all the means which made such a community possible were provided in his psyche and in his physical constitution. If we look at his sensory organs, it becomes clear that they were designed for union. The way in which one human being looks at another involves a preparation for contact and the expression of union with others. A person's way of listening indicates his possibilities for establishing contact with others; and his manner of speaking represents the bond he establishes between himself and his fellows. Can we now understand why so many human beings do not look, speak, or listen correctly? If we exclude organic deficiencies, then it is those people who fail in making contact with others. It is not the organs, not the instincts, but the fact that from the beginning of all psychic life, there exists a frame of reference, urging and leading people toward a social attitude.

Again, it is the weakness of the infantile organism which favors this contact. The infant's relationship with its mother is the first social training. All possibilities and all aptitudes are developed in this social relationship, where the infant's "I" experiences another's "you." Hence we can see that this gives rise to an important task for the mother: to guide the infant's development so that, later, one can expect him to respond correctly to the demands of social life. Once the framework is established, the infant will look, listen and talk in relation to his mother. This is the mother's first function. Mothers are at the source of social feeling; they should uphold it as sacred. Whatever develops there, develops continuously, hour by hour, and finally becomes an automatic, psychic mechanism; it shapes the life form of the child. If we consider the development of speech, that very important social function, we can understand where and how the community brings its forces to bear. "I must speak the way I assume everybody must speak in order to be understood by everybody else." We often find that where the mother failed in her first function, she did not succeed in her second one either, i.e. the extension of the child's social feeling towards others. We find a lack in the child's preparation in how to behave to others. This will be one of our most important considerations—this lack of interest for others in general. Since a feeling of relatedness has not been established, where will we now find a way to prepare the child to develop his social sense? This lack of interest has already taken on form and appearance; a goal exists for the child: to go through life without any interest in others; always taking and never giving. Here, already, a sense of worth.... Only a child who feels himself in his rightful place, will possess it. The child who has not made himself a part of the whole will never know it.

Of man's greatest faculty, his intellect, we must state here: There is no private intellect, no intellect of the individual. "Intellect has general validity". It has developed only by understanding others, by getting close to others by identifying with them, by seeing with their eyes, by hearing with their ears, by feeling with their hearts. *To understand* means to conceive of a man, or an event, in the way we expect everyone will conceive of these things. Here, too, we have as a companion the control of the community. I do not want to speak of morals and ethics as such; they are only rules from out of the community feeling. Only that which serves the community can we call moral or ethical. And the same is true of esthetics. What we call beautiful should have an eternal value for the community. It should not surprise us that we are subject to errors. We have always been ready to admit our errors, and to correct them. Even if a change in the ideal of beauty is a very drastic one, it is certain that the only lasting form of beauty is that which looks towards eternity, and conforms to the conditions necessary for the welfare of mankind.

I would like to call attention to the tremendous power of the social feeling for the individual—it creates communities big and small, and national, political or religious movements. To determine which of these forms are socially useful, we use the same standards; we recognize as valuable only those on the level of general usefulness. This, of course, is a subject for discussion and it is sometimes difficult to arrive at precise solutions for these problems. Human life is becoming. What we experience today is only an intersecting point in the eternal striving toward the goal of perfect form. What happens to those who do not act within the framework of society—those who give no evidence of social feeling?

In this connection we should note that what an individual says or thinks of himself is absolutely of no importance: we cannot attribute any value to it. The only thing we can evaluate are his actions. Thus a person may consider himself an egoist, whereas we may find that he is capable of altruism and working with others. On the other hand, many people may consider themselves as real "fellow men", but a closer examination may show us, unfortunately, that such is not the case. These are not necessarily lies; mistakes in the psychic life play a much more important role than conscious falsehood.

How do these errors get into the psychic life? Why is it that our impatient effort toward community develops so slowly? There are several answers. A large portion of mankind is possessed by the idea that there is nothing they can do, that human capacities are strictly limited. These are the pessimists who do not contribute anything toward the development which we consider the essential purpose of life; to help in the overcoming of difficulties.

I often tell my students this little story. "Let's imagine that our distant ancestors are sitting on the branch of a tree, perhaps still equipped with tails, and thinking about what can be done, since life is such a miserable thing. One of them says: 'What's the use of fretting about it? Things are just too difficult. The best idea is just to stay up here.' "

What would have happened if that one had won the argument? Today we would still be sitting in a tree, and we would still have tails. And indeed, what happened to those who stayed up in the tree-top? They perished. This process of extermination goes on continuously. It is terribly cruel; the logic of facts is cruel. There is no doubt that myriads of men were sacrificed because they did not come down from the trees. Peoples have been exterminated, families destroyed, because their responses to the demands of life were faulty. This process takes place under a kind of camouflage, so that it can rarely be traced. It may come to an end in the third or fourth generation, and no one knows why.

On closer examination we find that it is impossible to give an incorrect answer to the demands of the logic of human communal life without having to pay for such mistakes, whether it be in illness or serious physical or psychic degeneration. It becomes quite clear that these are the results of mistakes as Emerson expressed it saying that we want to avoid the consequences, but not the mistakes.

I have indicated where this process starts. Everyone takes a position towards life. It is only idle talk when someone says that a conception of the world concerns philosophy only and not each one of us. In each we can see his individual view of the world clearly expressed. For the person who realizes this, it becomes quite evident that he can only be helped if he develops a better conception of life. The question is: What conception of the world are we going to adopt to replace the one that seems false? In the chorus of voices you will hear advocates of conceptions of the world which are national, religious, European, Asiatic. We are not prejudiced against any of these. What we demand is that it take a form leading to a conception which includes social feeling; this is the philosophical conception of Individual Psychology. We are working to make this the touchstone because we have learned from both the individual and the masses, where they made their mistakes. We cannot agree with those who speak out for making things easy—who believe that everything is saved if difficulties are done away with. Social feeling itself is derived only from the arduous creative effort of each individual.

The mother is the indispensable mediator for life; she must bring forth social feeling, guide it and direct it toward others. But there are dangerous corners where the development can founder; for example, when the mother herself is not a truly social being, so that she is unable to develop the social feeling. Or else she may be a "fellow man" for the child only and not for others; she ties the child so closely to herself that she undermines his further development. These are the basic errors, but there are other dangerous phases in the development of children.

Children born sickly consider the world a vale of tears and display none of the joy of development which we appreciate so much in other children. We can well understand why these children, who are overtaxed, who experience their bodies as a burden and find life oppressive, are much more interested in their own persons than in others. A state of panic is created; every man for himself. These children show egotistical traits which hamper the development of social feeling. There are a great many such physically weak children; and this is not surprising, considering that the entire human organism is weak compared to other organisms.

Then there is a second category of children who are overburdened from the very beginning of life: the spoiled children who are interested only in one person, and who want to be helped by that person all the time. As soon as the style of life is established, in the fourth or fifth year, it no longer allows for any radical changes. Whatever they experience with this form of life is assimilated by them with *their* style of life; they see the world with their own eyes, they have their own conception of life—to be supported by others, they want immediate success, and fail when they have to make an effort. It is hardly necessary to point out that such children have difficulties and fail in any new situation. Spoiled children constitute a great segment of the population. I do not believe I am exaggerating when I say that from fifty to sixty per cent of all children have been made dependent. This lack of independence is manifested throughout all of their lives: everything is too difficult for them; they do not trust their own ability. American history contains an interesting example illustrating this case. In the Spanish-American War the Americans were allied with General Garcia. It was vital to send a message to him, but he could not be located. The message was important, and there was nothing else the American general could do but announce publicly that he had a message for Garcia and ask who wanted to carry it. After a long silence, someone came up, took the message and left.

Some American schoolchildren were given the assignment of writing a theme on the subject: "Who, in your opinion, is the greatest hero of modern times?" One pupil wrote: "The soldier who took the message to Garcia." And he explained: "Most people would have said: 'How can I find him?' or: 'Couldn't somebody else do it better?' But this soldier didn't say anything. He just left. He was independent. The others felt they were weak."

That is the source of all the defects in our souls—the excessive feeling of weakness, the lack of confidence in our own strength.

The third category of children consists of those who also feel overburdened from the outset, and cannot become interested in their fellows: the hated children. They have learned that there is a "fellow man". There are a great many such children: illegitimate, unwanted, orphans; and our culture has not created the necessary living conditions for them. Also, there are the ugly children, who soon learn that people are not well disposed towards them. It is easy to understand why there are so many ugly human beings among criminals and drunkards. There are also handsome individuals in this group—but these are the pampered ones. They represent a big percentage of individuals with problems, and they betray by their behavior that they have no interest in others. These are the problem children whose conception of life is: Let my will be done. They fall into petty thievery, they run away from home, they don't work. They deserve pity, because everyone feels that they are not "fellow beings." What happens when they are confronted by more important tasks? It turns out that they cannot participate in life. Neurotics and insane ones try to break out of the framework of society because the tasks of living seem insurmountable to them. They too, manifest a conception of the world, one which says: "I need another planet where there are no chores—where you find everything you want." Criminals too, who show no interest in others, are individuals guided by the idea that they can attain superiority easily without regard for anyone else.

In all these groups we find a lack of courage in facing up to the tasks of life. They are fugitives who want things to be different and easier for them. They do not try to create the conditions which are necessary for solving the problems of their lives.

Next come the candidates for suicide, who show us how little interest they take in cooperation—how little courage they have for facing the tasks of life. Mere statistics cannot convey the total evil. Just let the price of grain go up, and you will have more suicides.

Or create unfavorable living conditions, and you will find a huge number of people inclining toward the anti-social side of life. The tendency to escape from the useful side is tremendously strong.

There is no ideal development of the social feeling; we must keep the goal before our eyes, not for moral, social charitable motives, but for scientific reasons. We see that mistakes always backfire. This also applies to nations when they lack the courage, when they do not have enough interest in others, to protect against wars. World history is a chain of such unhappy events.

I will not go into the question of alcoholics, but before concluding, I would like to touch upon a point which will show how important it is to develop social feeling. In our life, there are no situations that do not demand the development of social feelings. (Earlier, I alluded to the functions of the sense organs). It begins with the child's relationship to the family and to the relationship with his brothers and sisters. When the child begins to go to school, he is tested for the degree of his social feeling. When the problem of comradeship develops, the question arises: "How far have you been prepared in your interest in others? And we can see that the lack of social feeling takes its own vengeance, for without it the individual cannot take his place in society.

But we also see that he is not responsible for it. We must think of some other remedy than those employed up to now. There is also the question of occupation, and the question arises: "How can I make myself useful in work?" There is no occupational activity that is not useful to others. The problems of love and marriage also demand a developed sense of interest in others. Again we see how deterioration progresses when the individual does not feel attached to the community. This is manifested in the choice of the partner, whether someone wants to dominate him or feels intimately united with him. And there are so many other problems, but all of them demand social feeling. The same applies also to the life of nations. A nation cannot progress unless it takes an interest in the world community. If it puts its egocentric interests first, another nation will remonstrate. I think that the results of the observations of Individual Psychology show that it must be to develop ourselves, and our children, to become the instruments for social progress.

Exaggeration of Self-Importance

In order to explain the methods of an Individual Psychologist, I would like to show you the way I proceed when dealing with the history of a problem child, a neurotic, or a criminal, in trying to discover the basis and real causes of his erroneous ways. We will find that everything which happened did not have to happen in such a way necessarily, but, under the circumstances, *could* happen; and, if we are able to feel with the child, to think with him, and conclude that under the same conditions, and with the same mistaken goal of a *personal* superiority, we would have acted in much the same way. With such an approach, a good deal of what previously appeared to deserve punishment disappears, which is by no means to be regretted. Our understanding and knowledge are increased, and, most important, we can recognize the connection between the innermost essence of such a child or adult, and his style of life.

To give you a correct idea of our approach, I would like to discuss a case with which, up to this very moment, I was not familiar. I have no previous notion of the events described in this case history, and shall try to follow the same procedure which I usually pursue in my practice. I may very well, at first, make an error in interpretation which will come to light later on as the case unfolds. If so, it will not discourage me. I am aware that I am in the same position as a painter or sculptor, who at the outset does whatever is suggested to him by his experiences and skill. Only later on does he check his work, strengthening, softening and changing the features to bring out the correct image. At this point, you can see that we proceed quite differently from other psychologists who would like to apply almost mathematical values and who, when their calculations do not come out, try to find causes in heredity, a dark area which can accommodate almost anything. Or they lay the blame on organic processes (a domain no less obscure) or on other factors which can scarcely be checked and which mark, to their eminent satisfaction the end of psychology. We do not avail ourselves of such methods. We prefer acknowledging our mistakes. At the same time, we have a better idea of the connection between particular traits and the total person; this is our advantage. It has become possible for us to draw conclusions about the whole from small details, as in natural history one gains information about the specimen from one little bone, or as one deduces the architecture of a building from one small corner of a window. And yet we are more prudent than those who try to describe and understand the life picture according to their prejudices. We proceed critically by tentative suppositions and their corrections.

When I begin to develop the history of a case with which I am totally unfamiliar, I am aware that perhaps two weeks later I might emphasize certain traits more sharply. But I also know that like all trained practitioners of our circle, I will arrive at identical conclusions. It is significant that we know this for certain, though we may use different words, choose different images, and even emphasize different things at times. But for us, consideration of the unity of personality always remains the most potent resource. We know that every child begins with a feeling of inferiority and tries to compensate for it; that he tends toward a goal of superiority, totality, that he sets about deploying his powers in order to be able to cope with all difficulties. We differentiate however, whether this striving is directed toward the useful or the useless side of life. The useful side is that of the common good, which follows the highest level of "common sense," where development and progress prove valuable to society. We try to locate the obstacle which caused the deviation; we try to find the problem which proved too difficult. We can trace the reverberations of these difficulties in the attitude of the adult, we will be able to say: At this point the road of life was disturbed here. An attitude developed which indicates that the person might not have been able to cope with his difficulties. Our attention is concentrated on these problems which he avoided. It is clear that we cannot attribute much *courage* to him. And another question arises: How did it happen that, at this point, the individual felt unable to cope with life's problems? Why did he prove unprepared at this particular moment? Experience has shown us that it is always the child in whom the social feeling was underdeveloped, so that it did not feel at home, was not attached by social feeling to others. This made it easier for the child to hesitate, to stop, to avoid things, to be satisfied with a useless solution of the immediate problem, which in itself already contains damage to others.

I shall try to utilize and demonstrate our technique in the interpretation of such a case, which may go back ten or twelve years. I did not see the child, but I received the following description: "I am taking the liberty of submitting the following case to you with a query as to whether education can help such a case. The subject is an eleven-year-old girl, well developed, well behaved both at home and at school, who is now in her first year of Junior High School."

This note immediately brought a problem to mind: What can education do in the case of failures? How should such cases be handled? It is evident that one should talk to the child, give examples, and refrain from punishments, as we always do. Punishing serves no purpose: the style of life is fixed after the fourth or fifth year and cannot be modified except by the subject's own recognition of his mistakes and errors. What can one change by verbal means? Only errors.

If in this case we are dealing with an erroneous formation of the style of life, and if we are able to understand this error, perhaps our knowledge will enable us to persuade the child that at this point she is making a mistake which can cause only harm. It is impossible to make a mistake without this mistake coming to light at a later date. It may now be recognized that a mistake may take its revenge in the bad formation of a life process, but it will be experienced nevertheless. We want to recognize this; we want to establish the context and make it clear to the person. We want to convince him to the point where he cannot take a further step without this conviction. One often encounters the following objection: "What do you do when the individual has recognized his error and does not correct it?" If he actually recognizes his error—if he understands the connection and persists in his attitude despite the harmfulness involved—we can only say that he has not understood everything. I have not yet seen a case of this kind. *Really* to recognize an error and then not to modify it runs counter to human nature; it is opposed to the principle of the preservation of life. The objection concerns a pseudo-recognition of errors. It is not a fundamental recognition, where the social connection is actually realized.

If it is really a question of errors in the case we are dealing with, we can provide a cure through education. The child is a girl of eleven, well developed, well behaved at home and at school, and a student in Junior high school. She is in the grade corresponding to her age. We may conclude that as far as her case concerns a solution to the second problem of life—the problem of work—the girl is in her proper place. We cannot raise any serious objection as regards her occupation; and we can maintain that the child is not classifiable as feeble-minded. There is too much talk about this category, as if feeble-minded children abounded everywhere.

". . . When the child has to go to school in the morning, she is so nervous that everybody in the house suffers from it."

This happens often. The problem of school assumes undue importance. We can now understand the connection; on the one hand she is a good student; on the other hand she becomes very tense when thinking about the problem of school. But we could imagine the child afflicted by tension without making everybody else in the house suffer, too. From this we conclude that too little attention is paid to the suffering of the others living in the house. The child's nervous tension is explained not only by her way of looking at things, but also by her intention to demonstrate it to others living in the house. The child's nervous tension is explained not only by her way of looking at things, but also by her intention to demonstrate to others how important this terrifying problem is. Here we have the desire to prove to others what great difficulties she can conquer. And yet, despite the enormous difficulties, she is well out in front of her class. She overcomes her obstacles nevertheless. Let us see whether we can find further proof for this type who has such particular need to prove her power:

". . . As soon as she wakes up in the morning she begins to whimper and complain that she has been awakened too late."

Those around her must even participate in the process of getting up.

". . . She says she won't be ready in time. Instead of getting dressed, she sits down and cries."

Frankly, this surprises us. We would have expected to see this child get to school on time, but with many difficulties. Perhaps the case has not been presented properly. We were told that she is a good student. We may suppose that this remark has been tossed out to emphasize the significance of the case. I would like to question this—not because of my vanity as an author, but because I want to retain this doubt: I want to find out if the girl actually was often late for school. If this is the case, we will find out later. In our society it is hardly likely that a high school student who is often late is nonetheless a good student.

". . . In particular, she complains frequently about the way her hair is done. Nothing suits her—not even the way which usually pleases her the most."

This can be explained perhaps only by a desire to increase nervous tension by the ceremony of doing her hair. She wants to create a major disturbance for everyone around her, and in the problem of the coiffure she finds a way to do it. The question then arises why the child, with such ingenuity, comes upon something which aids her intention to create a disturbance for those around her? If somebody would now say "hair fetishism" he would employ a stilted psychology which lays down rules, and follows them by introducing a sexual scheme of strange words which do not tell us anything we did not know before, but which permit the secret insinuation of sexual overtones. Our psychology, on the other hand, has the warmth of life. It does not want rules. It is a creative activity: the recreation of a living being. Without going into any other interpretation, we recognize merely that this girl, with great ingenuity has discovered an important point which creates difficulties.

". . . The hours go by. Finally, the child runs off, without her breakfast, crying and complaining."

This situation is not rare, either; we find it often enough. If, before, I expressed a slight doubt as to the late arrival at school—if I thought it was perhaps an exaggeration intended to emphasize the suffering of those around the child—we find the confirmation here:

"The hours go by." One can hardly imagine that the time measures several hours. School begins at eight o'clock and it is unlikely that the child gets up at five o'clock. More likely, she will rise around seven.

". . . We tried to eliminate this last problem [doing her hair] by having her hair cut.'"

If we are correct, this serves no purpose. The child doesn't care much about how her hair is done: what she really cares about is creating tension in those around her. Her coiffure is only one of several possible ways of doing this. So let us see what she will do when there is no hair-do to worry about. If we had any doubts as to this girl's intelligence, they will disappear at this point. This is the test of intelligence and feeble-mindedness I recommend. If she is intelligent, the now more difficult situation will show whether she has ingenuity that we assume exists in intelligent children, i.e., whether she will find another means of accomplishing the same purpose.

". . . But that didn't accomplish much, because the question of her hair-ribbon immediately came up. And she began complaining in the same way about how her ribbon was tied."

This means she is intelligent; we are reassured.

". . . The fact that the child leaves for school without having eaten her breakfast must be noticed in class, because I can't imagine that a child could hold out, with an empty stomach until eleven o'clock and still pay attention to her work."

The final observation expresses the doubt that a child can keep going until eleven o'clock without breakfast. Now, if the child's real aim was to satisfy her hunger, it would be correct to say that she could not wait until eleven o'clock. But in reality, this child has another aim: she wants to disturb those around her with the problem of school. I don't know whether one should draw further conclusions. We can say this child is animated by ambition; she wants to be the center of attention, both at school and at home. Nevertheless, she is moving in the direction of general usefulness. We learn that she is very obedient at home. She has only one fault; she wants attention constantly. She seeks recognition, but in the wrong way. In the morning, when she has to go to school, her main idea is, "How can I make my parents see the enormous difficulty that is facing me?" This is what we may call, in our terms, "bragging."

If now we want to establish this child's degree of courage, we must say that she tries to present the solution of her problem as a heroic act. This does not show how much courage because at the same time without anybody's contribution and without anybody being aware of it, she is creating for herself a safeguard. If some day she should fail in school, it will be the parents' fault. This is a process in human life which deserves much greater attention. It is futile to label this process "unconscious." It is the mechanism of this process which we try to understand in its connection with life. We all experience it, but we do not give it a name. We can understand it only when we establish the context.

Thus we can now state: This little girl does not have much courage. We can also tell something about the development of her social feeling. No one will doubt that the torment which this child inflicts on her family bothers her very little. We realize that the only thing which matters to her is to be a martyr. All the difficulties she invents, even the fact that she goes without food until eleven o'clock are intended to make the picture more painful. She is strongly concerned with her own prestige, but not very considerate of others.

Perhaps we could draw further conclusions. But I am afraid that we cannot confirm them, since we do not have any other data. We could ask: What situation formed this little girl's style of life? What were the first impressions which marked her? What circumstances contributed to the formation of this style of life? She is an ambitious little girl, who wants to be a leader. If I were asked I would conclude that she is an only child. Moreover, considering the importance which the mother attributes to food, I would generalize and state that in this family food plays an unusually important role. We could go so far as to declare that we imagine this child as delicate and pale, because if she were robust and plump, the mother would not feel such anxiety. But all these deductions do not help familiarize us further with the image of this child, since we are formulating them only as an exercise, without being able to confirm them.

A few words on the subject of treating a child of this kind. This little girl enjoys dominating her family. She does not actually know this. She only *experiences* the suffering and the tension of others. This should not delude us. Does a millionaire think constantly of the size of his fortune? If one checked on this, one would only find out how often he becomes angry when everything does not go according to his wishes. This little girl is in the same state of mind. She *is* in possession of domination, hence she does not feel the need to reiterate it constantly. For her, it is enough to possess it. Thus we can understand why she follows this path without seeing where it ends, so occupied is she with the difficulties she encounters. But if she knew all that—if one could make her understand that she exaggerates this ordinary problem of school in order to "brag"—a great deal of progress would have been made.

It is possible, however, that she would not correct her errors even so. In this case perhaps one should go even further, and show her exactly what a braggart is. One would inculcate in her the conviction that the only person who brags is one who believes he is inadequate himself. The only person who tries to upset others is one who believes himself incapable, by his own actions, of proving his own importance. Perhaps one could also adopt the following point of view toward this little girl. "If you want to take my word for it, you are doing very well. But perhaps you should do even better. All this means simply that you are a very intelligent little girl who has found a good way to get her family upset." In order to convince this child one would have to explain other events and other memories. One would have to show her that all these tendencies which are leading to inevitable mistakes are due to her position as an only child. She should be told: "These are very ordinary things which often happen to only children." This would acquaint her with something she did not know before. This new knowledge alone would influence the complexity of her thought processes. It would be *obvious* that her actions were running counter to her social feeling. She would control herself, and the following would probably happen. In a few days, after having put her family into the usual nervous tension, she would tell herself: "Doctor Adler would claim that I do this only to make myself interesting." She would no doubt continue with this trick for a while. If such were not the case, I could help her to do it. Then there would come a time when, in the middle of a nervous crisis, she would remember the way I had interpreted her behavior, and beginning at that point several of her attitudes would disappear. Then a time would come when already in a waking state she would realize:

"Now I want to get the family upset."

This would be the simple course of such a treatment. Other approaches would also be possible. I myself like to use quite different ways. When I felt that it would be possible to speak in such a fashion, I might say: "School is the most important thing in the life of a human being. You should make even more of a to-do about it." By exaggerating, I would spoil her tendency toward acts of this kind." You should constantly make a lot of noise to emphasize your achievements and your self-importance, because it is plain to see that you cannot be satisfied to attract other people's attention by useful acts." There are hundreds of methods as Kaus says for "spoiling the good conscience". "Write this in capital letters on a note and hang it up above your bed: 'Every morning I am going to make my family terribly upset.'" She would thus be doing consciously, but with a bad conscience, what she had formerly done unconsciously, but with a good conscience. I have not yet seen that any one of my patients followed this last piece of advice.

* 2 *

A Student Repeats a Grade

When we discuss the life histories of problem children, we do not particularly aim at a characterization of a specific child. We want to consider these brief and insignificant descriptions as typical, and bring our experience to bear on them in order to see to what extent they depart from the norm, or again, in order to test ourselves in investigating the hidden recesses of the soul, and to determine the position which the Counselor should take when he follows the viewpoint of Individual Psychology. In reading these descriptions it should not be forgotten that we do not want to analyze any particular child in detail. The important thing here is to bring out certain points. We want to take an interest in them, and see in what life forms these difficulties appear.

"We have a report on a nine-year-old girl. She is repeating the second grade."

This information prompts us to inquire whether we are not dealing with a feeble-minded child. All we know about this child is that she is repeating the second grade. We do not know whether she repeated the first grade, how she usually behaves at school, or whether she was able to enter the second grade because of special indulgences. If such is not the case—if the child advanced normally from the first into the second grade—we can say with certainty that she is not feeble-minded.

A few words about feeble-mindedness. In our group the tendency to label a child as feeble-minded is rare—so rare that errors are sometimes made in the other direction, with the result that a feeble-minded child is considered merely difficult to teach. But this is a less grave mistake than to label a normal child feeble-minded.

To touch upon this problem rather briefly, I want to mention the current practice of determining whether a child is feeble-minded. If a child's intelligence level is two years below his own age, there are grounds for suspecting feeble-mindedness. We would also add that an extensive physical examination is advisable to determine whether the child has not been retarded in its brain development, whether there are changes or defects in its endocrine development, or whether the endocrine glands are not functioning normally and thus disturb the mental development. This examination should be made by an experienced physician. He will have to determine whether there has been a disturbance of the brain development, whether the child is hydrocephalic, microcephalic, Mongoloid, etc. (I won't go into a description of these conditions). It is only from the juxtaposition of these two factors that we can come to a conclusion and say: This child is probably feeble-minded. In mild cases of backwardness, these two methods do not suffice, and I usually call for a third examination, which is decisive if it is handled correctly by an experienced Individual Psychologist. The purpose is to ascertain whether the child has a style of life. Because, if the child has a goal which does not correspond to that of an approximately normal child, but if in accordance with that goal he proceeds intelligently, although differently from the normal, the child is intelligent. He has an abnormal style of life, but he behaves with the corresponding intelligence. This is called a "problem child."

We are going to try to classify the girl mentioned above in one of these categories. In this case there can scarcely be a question of a medical examination, and even less of an intelligence test. We regard intelligence testing with some reservation: none of us trusts it completely. And so, our task is to ascertain whether this child has a style of life.

"We are told that this little girl has particular difficulties with arithmetic."

Our experience tells us that such children are most often pampered children who do not want to function independently, because of all subjects, arithmetic demands the greatest degree of independence. In arithmetic, apart from the multiplication table, there is no security: everything depends upon free and independent combinations. We know that pampered children, in particular, are far removed from such independent thinking unless they have in some manner learned to do independent combinations. There is another type of child who, through certain protracted events is especially discouraged about arithmetic. Children of this type have had a poor start; perhaps they could not keep up in the beginning and have not been encouraged. They do not have an adequate basis, and are feeling quite hopeless. "I have no talent for arithmetic." If any member of the family shares this point of view, we deal here with an advocate of the theory of heredity.

And there are other causes. I would like to emphasize one: There is a very strong prejudice against girls. Girls have often heard it said that the female sex is not gifted for mathematics. We already know that we should think of the question of talent. As long as a child is not feeble-minded, we believe that he can accomplish all of his tasks, provided he has enough courage. We have not yet reached any definite objective when we learn that feeble-minded children don't do well in arithmetic. Many particular areas of mathematics are better understood by feeble-minded persons than by normal individuals.

"The principal of the school feels that intellectually the girl is not able to cope with the curriculum. He recommends that she be put in a special study group."

This is something we cannot argue about.

"The parents believe that the child is intellectually normal."

The parents' opinion is rather important. As a rule, parents are the first to notice any signs of mental backwardness, even in cases where they are wrong. I do not remember a single case where parents would have called a feeble-minded child normal. Therefore, we can agree with the parents for the time being.

"They feel that a lack of self-confidence is responsible for the difficulties."

I am inclined to support the parent's opinion. So far, all we have heard is that the child is poor in arithmetic. If she does fairly well in all other subjects, it means she has passed the test of intelligence. The fact that she is backward in arithmetic cannot under any circumstances mean that she is feeble-minded.

"The parents do not rule out the possibility that the child exploits her disability in order to gain attention from the family, who give her a lot of time."

In this connection we recall that at the very outset we voiced the suspicion that this was a pampered child. In her own way, she wants to maintain her favorable situation, and thus she tries to achieve her goal: to keep her parents occupied with her. If we can give credence to this exposition (and many facts testify to its accuracy) we can say that on the one hand she lacks self-confidence, and on the other hand she is constantly seeking for someone to lean on. Consequently, she fulfills the conditions we laid down when we assumed that she was a pampered child. Immediately we see that she has a style of life, that she has a goal: she wants to lean on her parents. We shall be able to establish with sufficient certainty that she is not feeble-minded. The principal is wrong: the child should not be put in a special study group.

"Her oldest and her younger sister who are both very gifted, try to help her." This throws new light on the position of this child, who is between two gifted and independent sisters. We can imagine just about what has happened. For a certain length of time this little girl was the youngest. Then, suddenly the situation changed. Behind her appeared a little sister who gave the impression of wanting to out-distance her. On the other hand, as the second child she has not suc-ceeded in outshining the oldest. Here our experience with second-born children comes to our aid. Their ideal is to surpass others. We can assume that she tried hard to do this, and that she attempted to achieve a more or less normal development so long as the hope of catching up with the older girl did not fade. But she did not succeed. She is to be classed with that group of children who have lost the hope of equalling the oldest child, to say nothing of surpassing her. She will grow up under aggravated conditions, living with a feeling that she is not equal of others. She has a stronger feeling of inferior-ity. If, at her back, the third child appears as a new enemy, the girl will soon consider herself lost. She will begin to despair, especially about things in which she does not succeed rapidly. This seems to have been the case with arithmetic. Therefore, the description of her attitude toward arithmetic is exactly what we might expect. She has lost hope. It is an attitude toward arithmetic which cannot succeed.

But where is this girl's striving for superiority? This striving does not get lost; in some way it is that characteristic of a second child. She isn't doing well in arithmetic, and probably not in any other sub-ject, either. She has to take a year of school over again. Put yourself in the place of such a child. As far as progress goes, she cannot compete, so she gives up. But she must find another way of surpassing her sister. The question is: Where do we see this striving? She can only succeed in some way which is no longer useful and which is aimed at gaining her parents' continuous attention. The parents have their hands full with her. She is the problem child—the center of attention. Our question as to whether she is intelligent, has been answered. If there are any doubts, let us put ourself in this child's place, for whom the road to the useful side has been blocked. What can she do, since hu-man beings can live only as long as they have hope of having some significance as an individual, as a person. I would act in exactly the same way. From this I draw the bold conclusion that this girl is acting intelligently in order to achieve a faulty goal. To be the center of the family is only a fictitious superiority—a goal on the useless side of life. Real superiority exists only in the area of social feeling, in the domain of common sense. What this child does is not common sense. The principal understood this correctly; and from it, he drew the mistaken conclusion that the girl was feeble-minded.

"Her behavior within the family is somewhat domineering and in social games she does not co-operate."

This is the kind of information we were waiting for. The child's striving has not disappeared; she is domineering; she tries to place everyone under her thumb. In a social situation, she will participate only when she can play the leading role.

A few brief words on the subject of treatment. I am convinced that efforts will be made so that the child will demand less attention from her parents, and make progress in arithmetic. But if she has already given up all hope of keeping up with her sisters in serious matters, of measuring herself against them in this respect, the only thing to do is to encourage her. In fact, this is the most important formula we have at our disposal. We cannot expect that her behavior, her domineering traits, her claims on her *parents* will weaken so long as she does not have a clear path to move ahead in a useful way.

We must open up a path for this child. I believe there are parents who without understanding this viewpoint, could achieve some success with this child. We would not doubt that she could be completely improved. I have said that this would be possible even if someone had a completely false conception of the child and based her problems for instance, on infantile sexual development. An approach based on such theories could nevertheless encourage the child even if only by showing her that her problems are interesting enough for someone to be concerned with them. He can chatter all he wants to, provided only that this one ray of encouragement enters the child's soul. The child will move ahead without knowing how, while the doctor who treated her will swear that his method is the right one.

We maintain that we must encourage the child. This is not an easy thing to do. What should we do to accomplish this? We must induce the child to become more independent; we must convince her that she can solve her arithmetic problems; we must see that she acquires self-confidence—that she fills the gaps in her knowledge. It is not enough to give her courage in words; it is necessary to bring the child up to the standard of her schoolmates. If she begins to work, and has to take a test a week later, there is no doubt but that she will fail. The gaps are not filled that quickly. One must evaluate how much time is required for this purpose. In the meantime, she must be allowed sufficient time, during which she should not be made to take an examination as if she were already as far advanced as the others; otherwise, all the teacher's efforts will have been wasted. If this is not done, it will be desperately difficult to encourage the child again. When one tries to encourage a person, one must first create a state of mind which induces confidence. One must get him into a receptive mood; that means one must gain his confidence first. One must treat him as a friend. One must not show superiority and thereby crush the child, nor should one be harsh. These children have been treated harshly, with the final result that they feel justified in ceasing to work. It is necessary to bring them into friendly relation with the teacher in order to increase the circle of people in whom they have confidence. The girl in question has confidence only in her parents. At school she plays a poor role. Actually, her striving is directed only toward her parents. If a stranger succeeded in widening the circle of people she trusts, her social feeling would be augmented and her confidence would grow. This would remove the greatest stumbling block: The child's feeling that it has no place in the world, outside the circle of her parents. This process of winning her confidence should precede all other measures. We find ourselves back at the source of education, where it was the mother's function to gain the child's confidence and to awaken his interest in others, an interest in the problems of life, in order to create for him a place within society. This gives the child courage and independence and a feeling of equality.

If we now look back to discover the mistake which created the child's seeming disability, it becomes quite apparent: the two sisters, between whom this child stands, are said to be very gifted. This is not a one-time statement only: it is something that is experienced every day, every hour. This patient constantly has the impression of not being the equal of her sisters. Here her basic error appears clearly. I cannot decide why the other two show themselves to be gifted; but I can say that the first child bore up under the tragedy of having a sister because she has a solid position during the period preceding the second child's birth. I can also say that the second child did not bear up well under the birth of the third child. If we add to this the character of the youngest child, who is ambitious, you will be able to understand that the second child, who was already discouraged was again damaged by the birth of the youngest. We pose the question: Where was the mother? It would seem that the two other children were given a larger portion of maternal tenderness. The second child's attempt to draw all attention away from the others to herself is resented by her mother. The mother also did not succeed in teaching the second child to take an interest in other people, in her sisters, or in the tasks of life. The girl has remained in a state of dependence like that of her infancy; even today she shows the traits of a helpless infant.

Second case: "A girl of nine is repeating the third grade."

Again, we see from this one communication that if this child was promoted rightfully to the third grade, she, too, is not feeble-minded. Some things must have happened so that this child can no longer progress in school. The girl must feel that school is no longer a pleasant place to be.

"Particular complaint: a tendency to lie and to steal."

With respect to lying and its psychological structure, one can say that, obviously, there is somewhere in her environment a firm hand feared by the child. Normally, all children would tell the truth if they felt strong enough. We arrive at the conclusion that the child feels ill at ease. I beg you to consider that when you hear of a child's tendency to lie, it is a form of expression of a feeling of weakness. It is a compensation in order not to feel inferior, not to appear weaker, not to be the one who must pay others, not to be forced to consider others stronger.

There are two basic forms of lying. The first is the lie told out of fear. Fear is an aspect of the feeling of inferiority. When a person feels strong enough, he has no fear. The second is the type of lie wherein someone tries to appear bigger than he believes himself to be in reality. This is likewise a compensation for a feeling of weakness and inferiority. The tendency toward fantasy develops from a great weakness. If by chance someone wanted at this point to distinguish between lies which serve a definite purpose, and other lies, he would be on the wrong track. There are no lies without a purpose.

Now we are going to look for the firm hand mentioned. When we are told about the stealing of this child who seems to have a strong feeling of inferiority and who has a tendency to escape the superiority of others by devious means, it strengthens our concept. The psychological structure of stealing is one in which someone feels impoverished and tries to make up for this deficit by enriching himself. He does not do it in a way appropriate to the useful side of life, but by a trick which is very much like lying. Stealing is also an attempt to outwit the stronger person—to equal him through cunning. I have already shown that we can never find courage in those who steal. We see the characterological aspect clearly: the child here manifests her cowardice. We are not in a position to say whether another child in the same situation would not lie too, but we know with complete certainty that if this child would feel strong, we would not understand why she lies or steals. If she nevertheless continued to lie and steal, we would consider her feeble-minded. We gather that this girl must have a pronounced feeling of weakness, and that she is trying to emerge from her situation by employing means typical of the weak.

But the child behaves intelligently. This goes so far that we could, under certain circumstances, pardon a lie because we saw that it was appropriate to its goals and we can forgive a human being for stealing, but unfortunately only when he is near starvation: Then we would find it even justified. We must observe everything in its interconnections: lying and stealing are our first observations and we have concluded that she feels ill at ease.

"Her parents have been separated since the end of the war."

We often find this in the case of problem children.* The mother did not succeed in gaining the child's confidence: she failed in her first function. We shall now see whether this child turned toward the father. The affectionate relationship between the child and the father is always a second phase. Prior to that a break with the mother must have occurred. This can happen only if the child has the impression that the mother has not been a real friend. Frequently a child may

---

* Quarrelling parents are bad for a child's development, and we see from statistical and personal experiences that children whose parents are separated progress poorly; we find impressively many severe cases of failure. "She was given the option to remain with her mother but did not want to". We are reminded by this statement of what we had said before.

be unjustified in so feeling. Many children turn away from the mother when a second child arrives, because they consider this an act of betrayal; and they become critical of the mother. This is often the beginning of a faulty development in forming the style of life.

Let us now see whether the father has replaced the mother in her functions. In the case of a broken home this is not easy, especially when we are told that the father does not have much free time. Then what is left for the second function; the development of the social feeling? We are told that the child steals and lies. This is a sign that she has not developed a high degree of social feeling; that she has been growing up as if in an enemy country. When we learn that she has failed in school, and that she had had to take a year of school over again, we understand that this will not add to her fondness for her teacher. You can see that if this child considers other human beings as enemies, she is caught in a trap from which she never can escape by her own powers. Her distrust and animosity toward others means that she does not have friends, that she does not look at new situations with any degree of hope, that she cannot find her way in school. All of this leads the child to experience failures which reinforce her belief that life is indeed full of hostility. We can imagine that it will be very difficult to find a bridge to this child. Many will be discouraged.

This is what we can say from the material available so far; and we are waiting for new evidence to confirm or contradict our findings.

"The mother always treated her with very little affection."

We learn what we might have expected.

"She treats the child almost with distaste. The child is very attached to her father, although he often punishes and beats her for her wrongdoing."

In a way, this seems to present a contradiction. We should not forget, if we are on the right track, that this child has only one person in the world in whom she has confidence—at least partially. This is why the beatings do not particularly impress her. If the father abandoned her, she would have no one. Apart from the punishment he inflicts on the child, the father would seem to have his good points, so that the child sees him as more attractive than the mother.

"At such times she promises to behave better; but she always falls back into her old ways.

Let us suppose that after being punished, the child does not prom-

ise to behave better, or that she would see that she does not want to
behave better. What would the result be? She could not play this
game; the father would lose all hope. All children and all adults sense
automatically that there is nothing more to be done with a hopeless
case; that a hopeless case represents the greatest danger for himself
and for others, because he has discarded all social feeling. In practice
this means: If I make my father lose all hope, he will throw me out.
But she falls back into her old ways. We are less surprised by this
than the father is, because we know that the child feels deprived; her
goal is to enrich herself. She feels inferior; she does not dare to tell
the truth. We should not overlook the strong threads that connect
the school with the home. We would like you to imagine the effect
that would be produced at home by a bad grade. When we give a
poor mark, the matter does not stop there. It continues; perhaps the
child will be punished at home, or will be consoled or the teacher
will be blamed—all consequences which we cannot approve of from
the viewpoint of Individual Psychology. Why we are in favor of doing away with marks, because one cannot foresee what damage may
result from 'them. It is easier if the teacher takes the family situation
into account when giving out marks; but in this case the grading system no longer has any reason for being. If the child is burdened with
bad marks, he will have a bad time at home.

"For reasons having to do with his job, the father could not keep
the child with him, but turned her over to her grandparents. The
grandparents, however, did not keep her for very long."

We have often seen that grandparents are indulgent and gentle
with children. This girl was born under an unlucky star; even the
grandparents failed her. Moreover, the reputation which follows this
child—as well as precedes her—probably is extremely bad and is
wide-spread. This creates a new difficulty. The child, whom everyone
regards with hostility, actually experiences that hostility. You can
see the trap in which the child is caught. You can understand how
hard it is for her to get out of it. You know how difficult this would
be for adults, therefore, what can we expect of children?

"Then she went to live with foster parents at—where her own
parents also live."

This event we also cannot see as an improvement of her situation.
She doesn't want to be with her mother; the father has no time. She
is living with foster parents, and feels dispossessed because she has

been robbed of the only human being in whom she has confidence. She sees herself deprived. In addition, she is forbidden to see her mother. This is one of the gravest mistakes to make a child's relations with one of her parents impossible or difficult. There may of course be reasons which justify such a prohibition; for example, criminality or overt immoral conduct. But the person who possesses the influence should see that the other person is not attacked or deprecated. Such deprecation is harmful to the child, since it leads to the belief that his ancestry is bad and that he might have inherited the traits of the person who is being deprecated.

"Despite this prohibition, she visited her real mother, stole money from her, and used the money to buy sweets which she handed out to her schoolmates."

This practice of giving away stolen money or sweets is a striking manifestation in thefts committed by young children or adolescents. It evinces a need to brag, to make oneself bigger. The other aspect of this attitude appears just as clearly. It indicates that the child wants to make herself liked. When we hear that this child who feels herself deprived makes gifts to others, then this is a trait which we must interpret as if the child was looking for the affection which her mother denied her and which her father gave her occasionally; but her getting affection appears to her gravely threatened. She is also a poor student. What can she do to be esteemed? There is nothing left but to bribe other children. And that is what she is trying to do now. She is seeking affection and love. Perhaps this is the strongest drive in this child: to make herself liked by stealing and giving gifts to others, then she feels richer. This, too, is the method of the weak one. She is a child who does not have enough self-confidence to hope she will be loved by someone. You can find this also among adults.

"She behaves in the same way with the proceeds from selling eggs. She stole the eggs from her foster parents and took them to her teacher, who wanted to buy some."

She plays the role of the one who provides her teacher with food. We do not know whether she did not want to make a present to her teacher; perhaps she really did take money for it. In any case, she was able to render a service. She certainly would not have known about the teacher's desire, if the latter had not expressed it.

"They learned about these misdemeanors at school, and since then she has been shunned. The foster parents do not want to keep her any longer, since they have discovered several thefts, mostly of food."

We do not know what she did with the food. Perhaps this child, who feels deprived experiences hunger in a particularly strong way because the feeling of loneliness is mixed in with it. A person seated in front of a full plate will experience hunger much less than one who has nothing in front of him.

"The situation at T—— is untenable. The father would like to send the child away."

You see the effect of the trap.

"The father is penniless."

From this we draw the conclusion that the child is not in a good situation also as far as food is concerned.

The following comment is very significant:

"Because of the mother's lack of affection and the judgments made by everybody around her, the child is in opposition to everybody. Her misdemeanors may be partly the expression of her inner revolt. In any case, because of this situation the child's adaptation to society is made more difficult."

You have there a perfect example of the third type of children with a pronounced feeling of inferiority: the detested, the illegitimate, the unwanted children, the orphans and cripples. In the case of all these children we can very often observe that, rightly or wrongly, they feel themselves hated. We have to correct this error; we must make it clear to the child that, even if he is right, he has no reason to believe there are no friendly and accepting people in the world. In the case of this child the feeling is somewhat milder because her father is concerned with her. However, there is not much he can do. His last resort is to give the child away. And she must have felt this. The child must always have felt very deeply that her father will not extend himself very far for her. This is why she is caught in a trap in which everyone appears as an enemy to her. Her social feeling cannot be developed. Thus we see certain symptoms appearing in the foreground: lying and stealing as the beginning of crime.

We also note something else, which makes the case appear somewhat more favorable. This child is seeking affection; hence it should not be too difficult to gain her confidence. This first function of the mother must be awakened. She must be freed from the wrong impression that man is bad by nature. These omissions in her background must be made up for. Having outlined an approach for treatment, we must add that the child must be rescued from her difficult situation.

"The child gives the impression of having a great need for affection and security." This confirms what we hypothesized about the child from the first bits of information we had. The child is seeking, but has not found: her courage has not yet collapsed.

In conclusion I would like to share with you a thought which came to me while reading these lines. Let us consider the following: This child, from an impoverished background, cold, hungry, without hope, without any prospects, grows up, looking for love and affection. What will become of her? There is no one to protect her, no place where she feels secure. She will succumb to prostitution.

Let us assume that she loses confidence and despairs of ever finding anyone who takes an interest in her. When she grows older, she will find a man who will court her favor, who approaches her with the impression that he will give her affection. This happens often, and for the most part it leads to prostitution. Let us assume that this child has lost the last hope of finding someone who will accept her. She no longer believes that she can find affection; she can't get anywhere at school; she has no home; she roams the streets. By accident she can easily make contact with a gang and start on the road toward crime. Or else she may do something on her own, seeking what seems to be an easy way of making money. She has been conditioned for one form of crime, and she may very well continue. Finally, deprived of any other possibility, she may become a habitual thief. Then the judges and the court psychiatrists will arrive at the conclusion that it is very difficult for criminals to improve, so, more severe punishments must be inflicted. She will despair of finding any way out. She will steal, perfectly aware that she will go to prison if she is caught. She is hypnotized by the delusion that she will not be caught. If, however, it does happen, she will go to prison, where she will be in contact with other criminals who will teach her more tricky devices. Once she is released, her situation is possibly even worse.

Thus, how can there be any improvement? Does anyone believe that encouragement can be given under these circumstances? It is impossible. Help could only be extended if there existed a service which would provide what we consider to be necessary: encouragement and teaching her to understand her errors. If there were such a service, the child could be helped. Of course it might happen that some teacher to whom the girl is entrusted might accomplish incidentally and without actually understanding the child, the most important task, and that is: give her courage.

* 3 *

A Father Prevents the Development of Social Feelings

The report I am now going to discuss is unusual because of its special brevity. If I endeavor to interpret it, I do so because, usually, I do not have more detailed reports available. We must learn to make observations on the basis of brief reports. It would be well if the art of drawing up reports were practiced more extensively. If this were done, I would have an interesting proposal to make; namely, that a detailed history of a problem child, a criminal, a neurotic, an alcoholic, etc., be sent to eminent representatives of various schools of psychology, with the request that they interpret the case and indicate the means they recommend for treatment. The confusion which today obscures modern psychology would be dissipated very rapidly, and a great many authors who ordinarily do not present themselves in an exactly modest manner, would suddenly go into hiding. It will probably be a long time before this proposal is realized in practice. We want to utilize this time to train ourselves in the art of interpretation of cases, and in the art of reading such a report. We are resolved to find the means of avoiding or modifying the errors inherent in the structure of the style of life.

The present report concerns a boy six years of age who goes to the first grade in primary school. The introduction reads as follows:

"Before the child was living with his family. . . ."

This means that he was elsewhere, probably with foster parents or in an orphanage. The images of similar situations, favorable or unfavorable, appear already.

". . . he was at the hospital, and had lived with foster parents."

It would seem that the child is illegitimate. This is confirmed by the next sentence:

"He was born before the marriage."

Despite all the progress of our legislation, this situation is not a matter of indifference. Because even if legislation went so far as to put illegitimate children on the same footing with legitimate ones a child like this would still spend the first part of his life with foster parents. This fact alone leaves a deep impression on a child's life, not because his environment is worse than it would be with his own parents (in fact, it is often better), but because it is very significant for the child, since we believe that the general social attitude toward illegitimacy does not keep in step with the progress of legislation. Even today I would like to warn all of you not to come into the world as illegitimate children.

"Living conditions: the parents are very poor."

This makes us think the child is with his own parents; it was only that he was born before the marriage.

"They get along as well as they can by selling newspapers. The parents and four children, aged one, two, four, and six years, live in one small room. At night they have only two beds available. The boy is the oldest child, and sleeps with his father. The father reportedly has a lung condition, suffers from asthma, and cannot sleep at night. At such times he becomes easily irritated with the boy, and beats him."

Thus the child not only has to sleep with his father; in addition, he is beaten. This is too much. Just one of the two would be enough. "Supposedly he shows little affection for the boy and prefers the boy's younger sister, who is four."

Once again we have a familiar problem: that of an older brother and a younger sister. We know that the boy's position is unpleasant enough *per se*, even if all the other difficulties were eliminated. We know that the second child is always engaged in a kind of competition, and tries constantly to surpass the oldest child. If the second child is a girl and the oldest is a boy, then this is even more the case. A second child who is a girl becomes somehow aware of the boy's privileged position, and wants to show that she is just as good as he— that she is the boy's equal and more. Nature comes to her assistance. Girls develop more rapidly than boys up to the seventeenth year. The boy does not know this, feels that he is behind, and accepts it as his fate. This is why we find, with remarkable frequency, that boys in this position are less active, soon lose hope, and try to get what they want by devious means. (Intercurrent situations, of course, can modify this state of affairs.) The boy abandons activity. The sister is different. She is prodigiously energetic and overpowering. When she meets with resistance she becomes stubborn, recalcitrant. Usually she develops well, is the better student, alert, and much more active. In most cases the point is reached where the parents say: "It's too bad that boy wasn't a girl, and the girl a boy." When we find with great uniformity, again and again that these boys end up badly, become delinquent, develop severe neuroses, and sometimes become criminals and alcoholics, one is obliged to say: What is the sense of all the talk about instincts? What sense is there in talking about innate mental faculties, when the oldest child always presents the appearance which is typical for him. and the second girl that which is typical for her? With correct methods we can change this, but we can prevent it only when we understand these critical situations and do not blunder into them with methods that are not justified.

"The child says that last year there were several occasions when he came home after midnight. . . ."

From our point of view, we can easily conclude that the child is probably not especially anxious to be at home; otherwise he would come home earlier. One has the impression that he is trying to put a distance between himself and his home. I have already analyzed cases of this kind for you. If someone goes away from home, it is an indication that he feels uncomfortable there.

". . . and that he was picked up by the police on five different occasions."

It is plain to see that the common fate of the oldest boy with regard to his younger sister was not spared him. In addition, his position at home is in reality very bad.

"He has begged in front of candy stores and movie houses."

This too, we can easily understand from his feeling of being pushed into second place. When he runs away and cannot even partake of the meagre food at home, what else can he do but beg? Or perhaps even steal. This would not surprise us either. Here we see then, in a pure form, the case which I discussed above, and which results from the relationship between an oldest child who is a boy, and a younger sister.

"Behavior at school."

This is something we can easily imagine. If the boy could show some good results, he could make some kind of escape from his destiny. But since he did not escape it, we can conclude with certainty that he is particularly bad at school—a black sheep. Let us see what the report says.

"The child comes to school dirty, with uncombed hair and ragged clothes."

As far as the ragged clothes are concerned, he is probably not to be blamed. With respect to the other points, I am sure that his sister will present a different appearance when she is six years old. At six the boy could already be able to wash himself and comb his hair.

"He cannot sit still."

Not to sit still in school?! That is a crime! In school one must sit still. If he cannot sit still it means that he doesn't want to be in school. At school, sitting has a different meaning than elsewhere in life: it is a social function. A child's social integration with school is expressed in this physical attitude. Thus when we learn that he cannot sit quietly, we deduce that he has no social feelings and takes no interest in the teacher, the other students, or school and its tasks in general. What does he do, then? I believe that with some astuteness we can guess.

"He strolls about in the classroom, sings while the teacher is talking, and mimics his schoolmates' answers."

Isn't this already a sign of his escape? But escape is not easy; certain threats appear. They will send a warning to his parents, and all the power of the police will be employed to drag the boy to school. There is no escape. This boy would no doubt have preferred to run away. He can still act up so badly that he is thrown out. And then he won't be running any more risks.

"He tries to start quarrels with his schoolmates."

Thus he shows an obvious lack of regard for others. This is also indicated by the following: "He jostles everyone he meets, and is particularly pleased when one of his schoolmates falls down."

Once again we see his lack of regard for others. We have every reason to wonder what will happen when this boy is ten or twenty years older. At school he has lived through bitter experiences, and likewise when he was begging. And he has no satisfaction at home. What will this mean later on? It is easy to guess. He is so far lacking in social feeling that there is only one way left open to him: since he is still somewhat active (he enjoys the misfortunes of others), and since he tries to annoy others, he can follow no other course but that of crime.

"Not long ago he almost broke a schoolmate's finger. He uses vulgar expressions fluently. He is alert, capable of answering very well when questions are put to him, and very good in arithmetic."

This last point should not surprise us. We can well understand that the boy has always had to calculate: whether he was going to get anything to eat, how much money he could get by begging, etc. In this way he learned to evaluate the price of things; he had to calculate. One can hardly speak here of an innate talent for arithmetic; he was simply trained well.

"But his penmanship is very poor; that is, when he will even write at all."

On this point, I would try to find out whether it isn't a question of a left-handed child. Because isn't it likely that this skillful and alert child is capable of doing everything well? There is reason to believe that in addition to his other misfortunes, he has had to bear the burden of a right hand which is inadequate (functionally).

"In drawing he has not got beyond the stage of scribbling."

This also indicates a left-handed child.

One more significant comment: "The child is of foreign nationality, which makes it impossible for him to be placed in an institution operated by the government."

He is not far from achieving his goal: to be expelled from school. He has almost reached it; the teacher, who was taken in by his game, is doing what the boy wants him to do. Since, unfortunately, he is of foreign nationality, we do not know what institution to place him in. It would be fine if he were reared in such an institution. But it is not at all certain that in such an establishment he would find someone capable of understanding the case. For twenty-five years we have been trying to make people understand the meaning of these reports on very young children, and their importance for the future development of human beings, but no institution has taken these data into consideration. If this boy continues to entertain the feelings engendered in him by his experiences—there will always be somebody who will get ahead of me; I will never be good for anything; I have to run away; I must try to get around the demands of life by means of tricks—he will enter this institution with the same automatic attitude and soon start playing the same game as before. Here, too, he will start off discouraged, not expecting to encounter an agreeable situation (for example, being a leader).

And yet, he would like to be a leader. He would like to have everyone watching him, and to be the center of attention. Moreover, he has succeeded, in a sense. The whole class pays attention to him. Nobody takes as much of the teacher's time as he does. He has in fact become the most important person. What he could not achieve at home, where his sister is the most important person, he has achieved at school. He managed this by craftiness; because his activity was aimed in an unproductive direction; because he set himself the ideal goal of personal superiority, and followed that goal. Now the entire government is concerned only with what is to be done with him. This is no small success. If the boy wanted to meditate on what is happening, he could say to himself: "If I had sat quietly in school, and if at night I had taken my father's blows without flinching, who would have given me any attention?" And in a sense he is right. We cannot deny it, and we must not forget it when we are preparing to do something for him. A counselor would not have any more success than other schools of psychology in trying to rid this boy of his striving for recognition. The child wants to be appreciated. This tendency cannot be suppressed. A way to the useful side of life must be cleared for this boy. We must strengthen his courage so that he believes in his ability to succeed in something useful. His misfortune is that he believes himself to be absolutely incapable. An adept of the Freudian school would say: These are atavistic instincts of the primitive society; the boy wants to kill his father. Since he doesn't believe himself capable of it, he is trying his luck with the teacher. The teacher will become so irritated that perhaps he will catch a serious illness which will kill him, and the boy will have attained his goal.

But the situation is quite different. The events in question are not the beginning of something, they are consequences. There is no doubt but what the boy would be delighted to play a role like his sister's. But this was ruled out for him at the beginning. This boy was not bad but good, like all children when they come into the world. He was prevented from developing his social feeling because there was no one to awaken it in him. Who is the person best fitted for this role? The mother. We are told that the child was first at the hospital, then boarded out, before he came to live with his parents. He was an illegitimate child. Two years later a girl was born, and she became the favorite. Who was there to tell the child that there exist other beings who are our fellow creatures? We do not doubt that he was capable of fulfilling the role of a socially useful being. What he needs is to find someone who will open his eyes in this respect. It is not easy, but it can be done. It is a matter of performing the first function which is normally the mother's responsibility, but which no one has so far performed for him. What he needs is someone to replace his mother in this respect, for someone to play the role of the person nearest to him in whom he can have confidence. Once this has happened, this person should assume the second function of the mother: to enlarge the awakened social feeling and direct it toward others. This would primarily be the father, of whom however we heard that he proved incapable of developing the traces of social feeling, had they been present. Nor could the siblings be of any help. Our art consists in replacing the mother and carrying out her second function.

I do not believe that any intelligent person could reproach us for trying to "guess" or having achieved a certain skill in this art. In fact, I consider it a prime duty to train my students in the art of guessing. Obviously, our kind of guessing should not be compared with the incidental guesses of someone unacquainted with Individual Psychology, one who believes that when he utters words like "inferiority feeling," "social feeling," "striving for superiority," "compensation" or "overcompensation," or "unity of personality," that he has "guessed" something in the sense we attribute to these notions. Such a person has merely glimpsed the keyboard; he knows nothing of the art of playing.

All great scientific advances were made partly by guesswork. If someone laboriously places one symbol next to another and abstains from any creative act, it is only sterile experimenting. What certain people call "intuition" may perhaps be the same thing as guessing. Especially a person who has studied medicine should not doubt that the art of diagnosis is actually guessing (exactly as in Individual Psychology) based of course on extensive experience tied in with an understanding of the laws of human life.

Using our experience as a basis, we can maintain that we are capable of drawing conclusions about the structure of the whole from small indications; that we can deduce the style of life from the footprints. We are not so much infatuated with ourselves as to draw firm conclusions from a few isolated words. But by further exposition of the report we can confirm our hypothesis or, on the contrary, see the necessity for making corrections. The former procedure is that of the expert in Individual Psychology; the second is that of the beginner.

On the basis of these reports, we are going to find out how far our understanding of these children can go. These case histories are incomplete, since those who wrote them up did not know exactly what we are interested in. Under these circumstances the difficulty is greater than if we had before us a child brought by parents who were able to give us information on certain particulars. In this case we can direct our questions toward the points which interest us. These points are: 1) What was the difficult situation in which these faults appeared? 2) What peculiarities did the child show previously? With considerable certainty we can arrive at the conclusion that we are dealing with a child who is inadequately prepared for solving the problems of life. Whatever the child may have brought with him by way of heredity is of no importance. Whatever was inherited does not come into play. When the child is not prepared in terms of social feeling, we can always discover a particular insecurity as soon as the solution of one of his problems requires social feeling. Now we are on firm ground; all that remains to be done is to discover why this social feeling did not develop fully. We will not find any people with severe problems, problem children, neurotics, alcoholics, sexual perverts, criminals, or potential suicides who do not demonstrate with complete certainty that they are afraid of solving life's problems because they were not correctly prepared in the area of social feeling. This viewpoint must be kept in mind. It constitutes the fundamental difference between us and other schools of psychology.

Revolt of the Youngest Child

"A girl four years old. She is not an only child, but she is the youngest."

We are sufficiently familiar with the characteristics of the youngest child. I will repeat, however, that because of his or her position in the family, the youngest child is constantly striving to keep up with the older ones, and if possible to surpass them. From the beginning, the youngest child has a marked feeling of inferiority, and hence will find it more difficult to develop social attitudes, and will have a greater tendency to disregard society in favor of personal superiority.

This does not mean that the child will fail automatically in the social sphere. When his hopes are not thwarted, the child can stay on the right track. But if he loses hope he becomes the adversary of the others. He will seek out the easiest path, trying to find devious ways. In life he will be afflicted with the envy of the dispossessed. He will show all of the characteristics of such a case, where there is no self-criticism, and no strong awareness of the importance of the community. If we remember the story of Joseph in the Bible, and those fairy tales which deal with the youngest child, we will understand that this is an age-old experience, that his style of life, his structure is influenced by the fact that he is the weakest. Nothing else plays such an important part. Whatever he might have inherited, by the law that has placed him in his position, he must play the role of the youngest child. This can be done either on the useful side of life, within the framework of the community, or on the useless side. For him the temptation will be greater than for the child who, during the first four or five years of his life, did not suffer so obviously from the fact that he is the smallest.

"She sucks her thumb."

This habit should have been dropped long before the age of four. (Of course all children may suck their thumbs occasionally.) The observations we can make immediately are the following: the child's parents did not succeed in making the child give up her bad habit by means which she found acceptable. If they begin to oppose her, they will find that she will accept the challenge. And the more they try to break her habit, the less they will succeed. She will try constantly to attract attention by her thumb-sucking. (A certain pleasure which spreads over the entire body may also play a part in this, since otherwise it would be difficult to understand why she puts other objects in her mouth as well.)

Wherever you find children who suck the thumb, it means battle. We can state this the more forcefully since thumb-sucking is not the only means by which children conduct the battle. If, for instance, the parents insist on cleanliness, a child will choose this area for combat, if the parents have not succeeded in building up a co-operative atmosphere with the child. Any child can be driven into opposition. If the parents place particular stress on feeding, the child will fight them on this ground. If they insist on regular toilet training, you will always find the child resistive on this score. This is one of the reasons why certain bad habits are retained. And the same applies to masturbation. Persistent cases of infantile masturbation always signify a battle.

Another cause, perhaps ever more potent, is certainly consonant with circumstances cited above. When a child has been dislodged from a pleasant situation, he will try in every way to recover that situation which enabled him to be the center of attention. Experience shows children that certain bad habits are particularly effective in attracting the attention of parents. Once a child has noticed this, it will be very difficult to rid him of a bad habit which, in his personal experience, has proven to be of advantage to him. In his desire to attract the attention of the family, the child will even accept punishment, as long as he feels he is the center of attention.

We shall venture to assume that this child's thumb-sucking is the result of her revolt against her parents. This revolt probably resulted from the fact that the child was dislodged from a pleasant situation, and wants to recover that situation at all costs. Of course, we will have to wait for confirmation of this assumption. But, it would suffice for me, *as a matter of practice,* to come to such conclusions. I am not forgetting that there are other theories concerning sucking. Freud regards it as a sexual act. Thumb-sucking and masturbation are the most accessible means for children. A New York physician, Dr. Levy, has conducted investigations along those lines, but he did not discover the slightest trace of sexual excitement associated with the act. He maintains that it is always a question of children who got milk from the mother without any effort, who did not have to suck because the milk flowed too easily. Thus their sucking apparatus did not have to be used, and now they try to put it into operation—which is why they suck their thumbs. It is not easy to understand why these children do not use their sucking apparatus in a different way, e.g., like those who suck their lips instead of their thumbs. We will have to wait for more precise results and extend the researches over a larger area.

Experience has shown that other explanations are still possible. For our part, we maintain the theory of Individual Psychology, namely, that this child is rebelling and wants to be the center of attention. If we are able to confirm this assertion it will be demonstrated at a single stroke that Individual Psychology has grasped a large part of the individual's psychic structure. If this is not confirmed, we will have to correct our opinion.

"She sucks despite all the steps taken to prevent it."

If she sucks, despite everything, the specialist will be able to assume that she is a child *in rebellion*. But some doubt could still remain. Perhaps she is doing it for other reasons, and she is *rebelling in order to* safeguard these pleasures. In any case, there is no longer any doubt that she is a child in rebellion. We cannot expect to see the truth of our hypothesis confirmed simply in connection with this one habit. Her life as a whole must show that she is a rebellious child, and her hostile attitude must be evident in every gesture.

"In most cases, especially when she is stubborn, she puts her finger in her mouth."

We have just learned that the child can also be stubborn. We think we can tell in advance that she couldn't very well do anything else. It is especially significant that she puts her finger in her mouth when she is in opposition. For an impartial observer this is a confirmation of our ideas and a contradiction of other theories.

"She vomits at the slightest excitement."

We are familiar with this kind of vomiting in children who are very skillful at refusing food. Let us not overlook the possibility that this child might have an inferiority of the digestive apparatus which has made it easy for her to vomit. Thus we see how the entire psychic dynamism has been involved in her combative attitude. The child possesses weapons of *attack*. Vomiting is one of them. If she were isolated and had only herself to count on, guided by hunger and love, there would be no need for her to vomit when she does not like something. Here the relationship to society appears clearly: when the child is not playing the leading role she becomes excited and starts to vomit, as though she wanted to accuse others and avenge herself upon them. This attitude represents a *social relationship* and signifies only that the child is rebellious, that she is fighting for recognition.

". . . when she refuses food."

This child vomits easily—a fact which cannot leave the parents indifferent.

". . . when she is being bathed, every order from her parents which does not please the child puts her in an extreme state of nervous excitement; screaming and struggling, she repulses all efforts to calm her."

This child is as much of a fighter as one could possibly imagine. If one had had doubts earlier and perhaps thought she was driven by hunger or love—by her "instincts"—when she screamed and struggled, it would now be difficult to accept such superficial explanations.

"For example, I tried to calm the child by telling her a story."

An attempt at getting the child's interest. We know how this attempt should be classified. It derives from the second function of the mother: to make the child participate and cooperate. When I stress "participation and cooperation," anybody who is not blind can see that this represents an attempt to bring the child closer to the community—a function which was disturbed.

"I did not address the child directly. . . ."

This is a device which we often use. We do it unobtrusively because the child, in her hostile attitude, does not react objectively but subjectively. She would go on the defensive, if she were approached directly.

". . . but I told a story to her sister, a girl of six and a half."

Now we hear about a sister, six and one-half years old, about whom there are no complaints. We may assume that she has become well adjusted, that perhaps she is liked better, that she surpasses the younger child and that the latter is trying to dethrone her. The device of addressing the sister was well chosen, because the younger girl tries to excel her older sister in every way.

"The disturbed child listened attentively."

It seems as though the child grasped the content of the story intelligently. But let us rather assume that this girl wants what her sister has; she *too* wants to listen to stories. We often encounter this situation with fighting children.

"She became progressively calmer, and toward the end she was very much interested in the story."

The cure has not been completed. This girl should be brought into the circle of the community, whose unwritten but obvious laws hurt her. We must strengthen her social feeling. It may be said that this can be done in a number of different ways. But it is the goal that one must not lose sight of: to make the child understand what we believe we ourselves understand, and to liberate her from her feeling of inferiority. These children sometimes show their feelings in the most whimsical manner. "I'm sad because I'll never be as old as my big sister." They lose the common ground of cooperation and participation, and tend to strive for the focus of attention in a personal manner. What matters is the relation of the individual toward society.

In this case the misdirection has been created through a lack of exactitude, through faults in education. I have the impression that prime importance was attached to food; the question of food was over-emphasized. I would advise the parents not to let the child see where the importance is being placed. When children rebel, they direct their attacks to those areas where they will bring results.

"Second case: an only child; spoiled. A boy three years old. During the first two years of his life his parents were very hard pressed for money. They could not even provide the child with basic necessities."

In this case, social conditions play a particularly bothersome role. The child perhaps does not feel them particularly, since he has never known anything else. But it shows that the child must have realized that life was difficult. Another possible factor is that the parents complained of their poverty in the child's presence and caused him to have dark apprehensions about the future.

"In recent months, however, conditions have improved considerably . . ."

A new situation!

". . . and as a result the parents tried to make up for everything in a hurry."

This of course means that they showered the child with all kinds of gifts, toys, indulgence, etc. We can easily understand that this is not a correct method.

"The child's parents give him more toys than he has any use for. He takes no interest in them; and in general he ignores all these things, showing no pleasure in them whatsoever."

One may suppose that the child has lost his interest by being overwhelmed with toys and sweets and that he has become satiated. The child takes it as a matter of course. It sometimes turns out that such children prefer to make their own toys and their own dolls, even if they are very crude. These toys usually interest them more than beautiful dolls that have been bought for them. This kind of education leads children away from society: they are being placed into a world where everything is presented to them on a silver platter, and where they have to make no efforts; such a world contradicts reality. Through the lack of interest which is now taking hold, it results automatically that this child doesn't want to be bothered with anything and is content to move within the limited framework provided by the attitude of his parents. He will not develop any activity, because he has not been trained to move by himself.

"The mother feels that the child is sensitive. Personally, I maintain that he is apathetic."

We will also accept this latter interpretation.

"He prefers to play alone. When he does play with other children he becomes either irritated or servile."

He is not used to this new situation, and it seems difficult to him; hence his irritation. Perhaps he is servile because he does not believe himself capable of initiative.

"When he loses in a game, he immediately runs to his mother."

He has no resistance. This, in effect, is the result of a mistake in his education. Through a series of defeats, this child has been removed from the workings of the community. He resents all situations as difficult. The child has been growing up without initiative, as though created for a situation in which everything is obtained without effort—a land of milk and honey. We can see the fallacy of this kind of education, in the sense that it blocks the child's path to society. The treatment here would consist in awakening the child's interest in others—in the demands of life; that is, in liberating him from his feeling of inferiority and inculcating a vigorous optimism which will make him understand that he can deal with all problems.

The Struggle of an Oldest Child For His Hereditary Rights

"A boy five years old; the oldest of several children."

In the case of an oldest child we are accustomed to finding an attitude which betrays his fear of being dethroned. He has a very good understanding of power relationships, with the result that he considers power the most precious thing in life and strives always to attain it. You will rarely find a man as concerned with the rules of life as is an oldest child. (The second child, however, is the enemy of rules and principles. He is an adversary of all one-sided power arrangements because he can imagine a different set-up. He will not be too much inclined to believe in the magic power of rules and laws of nature. In all circumstances he will have a tendency to prove that there are no fixed rules.) Thus we may suppose that this boy will have a highly developed sense of power, and that with a certain apprehensiveness, with a fear of being unseated, he will try to maintain this power, or to reconquer it. This is characteristic of the type who has retained hope. If he loses hope, he remains the same type, however, and expresses the regret and the despair of ever gaining power. He is the same type, but with less courage. We shall see which of these two aspects fits the boy in question. Both attitudes, hopeful or hopeless, feature a powerful desire to regain the exalted position.

We learn that this boy always wants to play the role of an adult, that he always wants to act as a model for his younger sister. This attitude is in accord with our theory.

"In every respect, the child belongs to the category of mentally normal children. He takes an interest in everything, and has extraordinary strength of will."

We must remember that this child is laboring, in a state of constant tension, to keep command—to keep the helm. This may seem to be a sign of a great strength of will, but we are not certain that a boy of five should be credited with such an attitude.

"He will manhandle children, and furniture, or even destroy valuable objects, whenever they are in his way."

This must refer to occasions when the child wanted to show that he intended to remain on top; and it proves to us that his social feeling has suffered. We shall see here not so much "hunger" and "love" as a striving for power. He does not suffer from suppressed excitement or experiences; his social feeling has been narrowed. This exaggerated striving for power is all the more understandable because he does not believe completely in himself especially since he has a younger sister. We already know that in the rivalry between brother and sister, the latter is favored because she develops more rapidly than the boy. Thus the older boy has to remain on his toes if he is going to stay in power when dealing with a younger sister. Other factors have probably played a role in this case; because the foregoing fact would not be decisive so long as the boy had not lost hope of triumphing over his sister. When he has lost his hope, he will resort to tricks. The older boy is a child who, at one point, was an only child. Subsequently, he ceased to be an only child, and he is not prepared for this situation in a social sense.

"The father told me that during a certain period the child was reared very strictly."

We do not know by whom he was reared—perhaps it was by the father. This would mean that he resents his father, and directs his attacks against him.

"The father maintains that as a result of healthy mental and physical development the child has an excess of energy...."

This is the stimulated urge for power, which the father does not recognize.

"... and this is why he is so exuberant. Up to the present time the child has had no childhood diseases."

It would seem that the father believes that childhood diseases have a beneficial influence on the development of character.

"In my opinion, this child is not to be considered 'inferior,' but ambitious."

On the contrary, if the child felt sure of himself he would not make such efforts. He is not "inferior," but he shows a "feeling of inferiority."

"His father is always held up to him as a model. He is a gifted man, with an attractive personality."

It seems that the father sets the tone, and this exasperates the boy even more.

"It is impressed upon the child that he will develop to the personality of his father."

This does not strike me as particularly difficult; but it seems so to the child.

"The father is an engineer, and has done outstanding work in design and painting."

Many parents believe that by holding themselves up as models for their children they encourage the development of independent judgment and action.

In this case history it is again a question of how far the child's social sense has been developed. All other considerations are secondary. This has nothing to do with natural science—with "hunger" and "love." Only the extent of the boy's striving for recognition is indicative of his social sense.

At this point I would like to add a few comments on an observation made by the teacher:

"Who is responsible for the fact that a five-year-old boy becomes agitated at the slightest provocation? Who is responsible for the gastric disturbances of the four-year-old girl? In most cases I have observed that it is the parents themselves who mistreat their children, not with brutality, but by their very tenderness clad in an inconsistent and illogical attitude. Only those who, in addition to the requisite knowledge, have a warm heart and a deep social understanding, are entitled to rear children."

I feel myself obliged to minimize the guilt of the parents, because if we succeed, for example, in improving these children—in cultivating a greater social awareness—the parents can no longer be blamed. Therefore, our social sense should be directed toward relieving the parents of this burden. This was the starting point of the practice of Individual Psychology, despite all the difficulties. We told ourselves: there is no official agency which could take this burden off the parents. We were aware that we could not accomplish this task by ourselves. We merely wanted to make a beginning and set an example. And we have received enough encouragement to continue along this way.

✳ 4 ✳

A Spoiled Youngest Child

"The girl is eleven years old. Her father is a retired railroad man; her mother is a housekeeper. The mother is reported to have had fourteen children, seven of whom are alive. Petronilla is the youngest child."

The character structure of the youngest child is very clear to us. You are no doubt all familiar with the biblical story of Joseph, who wanted the sun, the moon and the stars to bow before him, and who tells of his dreams, whose meanings are clear to his brothers. They first put him into a pit, and later they sold him. This legend is very instructive. Subsequently Joseph becomes the breadwinner for the entire family, the support of the entire country. He saves the entire population.

The youngest child! You will often find that in one way or another the youngest child becomes a prominent person, whether for better or worse, and often a valuable and powerful individual. We do not know anything about the sex of these fourteen children. However, we can affirm that the youngest child is often particularly spoiled because the parents are very pleased to have been able to procreate a child in their later years (unless, of course, they did not want it). The youngest child grows up in a different atmosphere from the other children, since he is the only one who has no successor. Hence his relatively privileged position. As for the others, they live through the tragedy of seeing their place taken by another child. The youngest child does not experience this, and it affects his attitude. He is not threatened by a successor.

We have the following information from the school questionnaire.

"She works willingly for a certain period of time; then her enthusiasm diminishes."

When you notice such instability in the work of a child going to school, you can conclude with some justification that the child is spoiled. He will make progress only under certain conditions, when he is in a pleasant situation, when progress comes without effort; when everything goes smoothly. As soon as the warm, comfortable atmosphere disappears, his productivity drops. From report cards alone we can diagnose whether such a student is a spoiled child. We are in the same position as a good practicing physician when it comes to a diagnosis of this type of spoiled child.

"The child prefers penmanship, drawing, and manual work."

This child is skillful with her hands. A certain manual training may be responsible for this, perhaps the child has had since her earliest infancy an inclination for doing things with her hands. We may perhaps also conclude that she is left-handed, that she has overcome this difficulty, and has trained her right hand particularly. But this second hypothesis must be considered with caution: it is easy to confirm or to deny.

"The mother defends the child's bad conduct."

Here we have a mother who defends her child even if the criticism is justified. In this way we obtain confirmation of the fact that the child is spoiled.

"It is easy to stimulate her interest."

This indicates to us that the child is interested in everything; that she sees and hears everything, and takes a healthy interest in life. She is a child who has not lost courage, who does not retreat, and who is not introverted, but who seeks contact with the outer world.

Here we will find a social activity which may be distorted only in a special area; but the material for social feeling is there.

"She tries to distract others by creating disturbances."

We could assume that this child is always trying to create disturbances in class. This does not surprise us, since we know that such a spoiled child, who has a certain degree of activity, will employ her desire to be the center of attention particularly on the useless side. Moreover, she will go rather far in this direction, since she finds a support in her mother.

"Remarkable memory."

Thus the least doubt as this child's capacity for lively interest disappears. I would not be surprised if an intelligence test showed her mental level to be above average.

"Observes daily events independently and accurately."

Again the fact is confirmed that this child possesses a degree of activity which prompts her to take an interest in everything, and to take a reasonable stand on problems.

"Sound ideas; critical talent."

We would not like to say that her critical sense always goes astray. However, although she is occasionally right, we will assume nonetheless that she has a tendency to elevate herself above others.

"Goes at all new work courageously."

We can deduce from this that at the outset of a new project she makes definite progress. Once again, we see her activity. We begin to see the outlines of this child's style of life. We have the picture of a very active child who takes an interest in the world around her and who certainly strives to raise herself above others. Now, in the social milieu of school, how will she rise above the teacher?

"Sometimes capricious in her work."

This is a repetition of what has already been said.

"The recognition that her work is well done encourages her a great deal."

She has an ardent desire for recognition; she would like to play an important role.

"She is gay."

This again shows us an aspect of her courage and her determination, as well as the fact that her home atmosphere is pleasant. We know that her mother defends her.

"Sticks to her own decisions."

Like anyone who feels strong.

"She distracts the attention of other children by disturbing the class."

When we hear that such a child distracts others in class, we know that she wants to achieve the goal of becoming the center of attention. The only way to do this is to disturb the class.

"Has a tendency to leadership."

The youngest child—little Joseph.

"But is not well equipped to lead."

Why isn't she well equipped? The other children oppose her. They don't want to be led and commanded by her. She has not yet learned how to lead others. But there is no doubt that sooner or later she will acquire the gift of leadership.

"Expresses herself well and talks easily."

Talking is another way of attracting attention. You will often find this love of talking in problem children, neurotics, and psychotics. Such people talk constantly.

The above comments had to do with the child's behavior in primary school. The following concerns her behavior in secondary school.

"Did not make herself conspicuous at the beginning. On the occasion of the first hike (an excursion with the teacher) some of her schoolmates complained of her antics and trouble-making."

She wants to be recognized. She wants to make a place for herself. But why didn't she make herself conspicuous right away? This would seem to indicate that her training was good: she had to find out how to do it first.

"For the past two or three weeks she has been behaving very badly. She shouts during lessons, constantly leaves her seat, jostles others, and tries to disturb them."

Her conduct obviously means that she proceeds in her efforts to outdo the others. We understand what she wants to achieve by this conduct: she wants to demonstrate her power; she wants to achieve domination over the other children.

"During classroom work she refuses to cooperate. When reprimanded, she became angry, seized the inkwell, poured ink on her hands, literally washed her hands, and soiled the desk."

The child goes beyond all reasonable limits and behaves like an enraged conqueror who is determined at all costs to show that he is the strongest. Since we are dealing here with an intelligent child, we can conclude that she feels ill at ease in school and that something more must be done for her. She shows us by her attitude that she has lost hope of playing an important role in this school.

"The mother is called in. Losing all control in her anger, she pulled the child's hair, senselessly slapped her in the face, and twisted her arm."

The mother also lost her self-control. We should note that this is not a good method for punishing the child's ultimate effort. The child doesn't care at all if she upsets her mother and teacher. I recently read a passage in a biography of Rosegger where the author relates that as a child he was filled with a great joy when he could upset his father so much that the latter beat him. Later on, having understood that his father loved him, he changed his attitude. The child wants the assurance that he is loved and that he is esteemed. When he no longer has it, he makes a point of irritating someone and driving him to his wits' end until the desired result is achieved. This gives him new strength.

"The principal quieted the mother with difficulty, and had the child go back to her classroom. The child did not cry, and did not shout: she controlled herself."

You see how she showed her mother: "You are too weak for me. I am stronger than you!"

"No sooner had the mother left than the child was sent back to the principal because she was making it impossible to carry on the classroom work."

She also showed that nothing could improve her—that "no one could influence her." In a way this child deserves our admiration: she is very strong. If one could channel this unusual strength into a useful direction, one could make something good of it.

"The principal talked kindly to her, and the child promised to be obedient. But at the very moment of promising she had scarcely any intention of keeping her promise."

The child realizes that the principal takes a sympathetic interest in her. She would like to please the principal, by being obedient; but in the classroom the mechanism of her style of life begins to operate. Some authors tend to believe that in cases like this we have an ambivalence: that the child is compliant in one aspect and disobedient in the other. But the human soul should not be represented so mechanically. Obviously, this mechanized style of life reacts according to its pattern; but it varies with the situation. In the principal's office the child has the impression: "This person has been won over: she belongs to me." But she does not have this same impression in the classroom.

"The principal gave her a responsible task: to bring the calendar up to date."

This is one way to calm a child at school, and it also has a more profound significance: it has an effect on children whose striving for superiority can be calmed by giving them a responsible task. But this child wants something more than such a task: she wants to be more than all the other children. And we don't believe that she will calm down for good.

"The teacher entered the classroom. The child remarked that the teacher had pretty curls, and wanted to know where she could buy them."

This signifies open hostility. It is plain that the child is engaged in an out-and-out struggle with the teacher. Only an avowed enemy can talk like this.

"The children in this class, ranging from ten to eleven years of age, were obviously too young to ignore such a remark. The disturbance continued. At first it seemed that the child wanted to annoy this particular teacher, especially, but soon other teachers came under attack."

It was perhaps impossible for this or any other teacher to give the child what she wanted: to be put immediately at the head of the class. On the other hand, we see that we can not do anything with this child unless we guarantee her right away what she desires. Otherwise she will drag us into the same struggle into which she has dragged others. It would be a mistake to reproach her with her faults. The thing to do is to begin a conversation with her in which her good qualities are mentioned. The way to handle this depends upon the individuality of the counselor.

"During two natural science lessons the principal had to remain in the classroom in order for the work to proceed undisturbed."

She isn't strong enough to challenge the principal. Moreover, she seems to be on better terms with the latter. This may be respect; but it may also be gratitude for having defended her against her mother.

"The teacher assigned a few tasks to the child: dusting off certain objects used in classroom work, and getting water. But once again, she very soon started to make trouble."

This prompts us to reflect. As we see, she does quite satisfactorily what the principal tells her to do, but if a teacher assigns her a task, she does it badly. Here, too, we can learn something; namely, how to approach this child. As I see it, modern education has a tendency to recommend a pleasant school situation; and one can abserve that in this situation a child behaves in a more satisfactory manner. Individual Psychology, on the other hand, tried to accustom the child to keeping his sense of balance even when he is in an unfavorable situation. Recalling the conditions under which the mechanized style of life is formed, we see that the latter is so constructed that the mother must provide the child with a pleasant situation in order to gain the child's confidence. She must then make the child a social partner in community life. There is no way of getting around this function which is incumbent upon the mother. We must start there and gain the child's sympathy, after which we must make her a member of society. If we do not gain her sympathy, we shall fail in the latter.

"During physical education exercises this student became unruly and broke out of line. She was shut up in the locker room where she proceeded to throw pieces of paper on the floor, followed by the other students' dresses. It was impossible to get her to put things back in order."

Always the same battle.

"Even the principal had to talk to her for a long time before she decided to pick up the pieces of paper."

Here, it is the principal again who persuades her to make amends and to humble herself.

"On one other occasion, in the locker room, she switched the shoes and stockings of her schoolmates. One child was unable to find her stockings, and little H was of course suspected. Neither the principal nor the teacher supposed for a moment that she could have stolen the stockings, since she is very neat and properly dressed. She certainly doesn't lack for anything, either in the way of food or clothing. The next day the principal, the mother, and the mother of the child whose stockings had disappeared, insisted that she tell where she had hidden the stockings. But she would admit nothing. Finally, after long searching, the janitor found the stockings in a ventilator opening just above the floor. But the child still swears she did not hide the stockings."

I feel it necessary to point out that the child does not show any tendency toward lying. In children who lie, we do not find such a degree of activity. Lying is a sign of cowardice. One must be prudent in such cases, since it is possible that another child hid the stockings. We can easily imagine how superior this child would feel if she were wrongly suspected, even once. I have seen cases where individuals had stolen numerous times, but had not stolen on the particular occasion in question; and the attitude they assumed when accused was farcical to behold. They made no effort to interfere with the investigation which was making them suspect; and they took pleasure in the injustice which was being inflicted upon them.

"Since the physical education instructor had refused to take any responsibility for the safety of the child and the other students, the principal was present during the lesson. She stated that the child's behavior was faultless in both the physical exercises and conduct in general. At the next lesson the child was praised; but she was already starting to attract attention by making faces. And she complained that her foot hurt."

This way of fighting is already much more subdued compared to what we heard earlier.

"The teacher says that if the child deliberately does badly at her exercises, she will get a low grade. According to the mother, the girl cried at home. Her mother consoled her: Don't let it worry you."

This is almost a case of a missed opportunity. It is very difficult to find a good opportunity to lead a child toward improvement. It may very well have been that the girl's foot actually hurt, and that she was already on the road to improvement. Then, her complaint is answered by the threat of a low grade.

"She was cooperative during the penmanship lesson, although even on this occasion she was once sent to the principal's office because she was making too much trouble."

She seems to be interested in penmanship. We had assumed that she was skillful with her hands, and it may be that in penmanship class she cooperates in order to outdo the others. We will see that when she cannot achieve this goal, she goes back to bothering the class.

"The teacher of geography, history, languages, and singing praised the way in which the child expressed herself; and during the first few weeks he remarked that she could take the 'A' courses."

Thus we learn that the girl is not in the "A" course. This is one of the most burning questions in educational reform throughout the world. In most countries it has been decided to establish two curricula: an "A" curriculum for children who are considered to be normally developed, and a "B" curriculum for those who give the impression that they are developing more slowly. The teaching in curriculum "B" is geared to children who are inadequately prepared, and one which provides them with an easier situation. But one must not lose sight of the weaknesses in such a program. I have the impression that children in the "B" curriculum always feel that they are below average. One often hears insults like "the dumb class," etc. It is of course true that some children will profit from the advantages of the "B" curriculum, but the disadvantages will weigh heavily on others. It is noteworthy that in some of my investigations I found that the majority of children in "B" curricula classes come from poor families. This means that these children are less well prepared for school than the others. The problem has not yet been entirely solved. The disadvantages of such a program have not been altogether eliminated. The question arises: how does the child feel about the "B" courses.

The teacher told her that she would be able to get along in the "A" curriculum. If we have really understood this girl's style of life, we can assume that she feels belittled because of being in the "B" curriculum. In this particular case the disadvantages of the "B" curriculum give us something to think about.

"Handicrafts."

This is also an area where she behaves according to style.

"The manual arts teacher states that in class she swore at one of the students, who was bringing her working materials: 'Slut, idiot, fool,' and other expressions which cannot be quoted here. The drawing teacher tells about a drawing he criticized. . . ."

Naturally, this is the watchword for us. Something is bound to happen!

"The child angrily smeared paint across her drawing and ruined it. The teacher tried to reason with her. Result: 'My father will come and punch you in the stomach! Maybe then you won't try to give me any more trouble.' "

"In catechism class. The child is Catholic, but does not take religious instruction. However, she sits-in in the class, and the priest called on her on several occasions. Once she was the only student there who could give an accurate answer to the question. She told her mother about this very happily. Then, during the next catechism class, the priest sent her to the principal's office because she was particularly bad in her behavior."

We do not know what happpened between the two classes. Once again, however, there was an opportunity for winning her over.

"Principal's remarks. When the child came to the principal's office she behaved in a particularly amiable manner. She was told to do arithmetic or to write. At the beginning all went well, but toward the end she was drawing doodles. When asked why she wasn't doing her arithmetic lesson, she said: 'I can't.' "

This is obviously a bad situation. When she doesn't know something, she has such a strong feeling of inferiority that she must compensate for it in some way.

"In addition to the honor assigned mentioned above (bringing the calendar up to date), she was given others: sealing envelopes and carrying messages between classrooms. On this occasion she seemed to be the sweetest girl in the world. But a few minutes later, despite her promise to be good, they had to send her out of class again."

The child has found the place that appeals to her: the principal's office. If she is sent somewhere else, she strives to get back. Her movement is in this direction because at the principal's office, she finds herself in a pleasant situation. It may be that the teacher actually has her welfare more at heart than the principal does; but the only thing that matters is how the child interprets it.

"The child says: 'My mother doesn't like "the older ones." She only likes me.' "

This feeling stems from the fact that the mother spoils her.

"Lots of times she brings me things. But not candy—just sausages or ham or pork."

"I want to be a teacher."

This does not surprise us, because in the image of the teacher the child recognizes a person of power.

"If I had to handle a naughty child I'd just beat him."

"I am supposed to go to dancing school. My sister said I could let off steam there. But my mother won't let me go. She says she can educate her child herself—that she doesn't need outsiders.

"I don't belong at X Street. On the list, I was supposed to go to het Y Street School. [This is not true.] I would like to go to the Y Street."

The X Street School has nothing to offer her. She has already shown everything she was capable of there. Now she feels she could shine more at the Y Street School. These are lies she tells in order to brag, bluff, and impress others.

"The child was sent back to the principal's office, and the latter asked: 'What have you done now?' She did not answer immediately. After repeated questions and exhortations, she decided to talk, and she told the truth. Once she lied to the principal. The physical education instructor reported that the child maintained that the instructor had pulled her ear, making it necessary to bandage the ear. The principal questioned the child, who stuck to her story. The principal explained to the child that her parents would believe her, and would demand an explanation from the teacher. (The child already had threatened that her father would come to school.) The teacher would then go to court, and her parents would be fined for having libelled her. At this moment the child admitted she had quarreled with her sister and the latter had hit her on the ear, which necessitated the bandaging."

This is a lie used as a fighting weapon. She wanted to "do in" the teacher. Here we are not dealing with lying out of fear. It is a slander, not a lie.

"On one other occasion she lied again. The mother had requested that her daughter be placed in the back row so that she would not disturb the other students. This was done. The next day the child came to school wearing glasses and complained that she could not see from the back row and should be put in the front row. The doctor happened to be on the premises, and examined the child. Having been informed of the case, he reassured the child and told her she was just nervous, and that she could get along very well without glasses. Now the principal questions the child more closely and the child finally admits that the glasses were her mother's. The mother gave a different story.

"The parents seem to have understood that the child is badly behaved, and they admit they do not know how to deal with her. The father says that the mother stands up for the child. The mother says that the older children often reject the little girl, and that she herself is the only one the girl can count on."

The problem of Joseph again. It is the same expression that we find here.

By way of conclusion, a few more items which complete the report:

"Report of the class teacher: During certain lessons the child behaves perfectly; then she goes back to disturbing the teacher. Most of the time her notebooks are in disorder, but she turns in her assignments and exercises in a satisfactory manner. She likes to be called on in class.

"During the singing lesson she is incapable of keeping with the others. She sings purposely faster or slower than they do, and is obviously pleased if she can bother us.

"Her lack of affection (she even takes joy in torturing her schoolmates) and her tendency to want always to play the leading role, are especially flagrant."

This is sufficiently clear.

"Pretentiousness, arrogance, conceit, spitefulness, and lying. Generally speaking, she seems to be quieter at the present time. Her spitefulness has somewhat diminished."

A slight improvement seems to have taken place recently.

"The manual arts instructor reported that the child was sitting on a chair, rocking-horse fashion, and making it go around the room. When the teacher threatened to tell her parents, she replied: 'They don't care. And I'm not afraid—not even if the mayor comes!'

"During the next lesson she imitated birds singing, and called the teacher's attention to her talent.

"She works at her arithmetic assignments—without, however, relinquishing the constant assistance of the teacher."

She wants to have someone at her disposal at all times. This is a trait of the pampered child.

"Once she made so much noise at the beginning of class that it was impossible to continue teaching the lesson. She ran around in the classroom, hitting other children and insulting them. At one point she shouted: 'I'll stick a knife in your ribs!' Nor did she become more cooperative later on. She kept saying: 'I can't do that.'"

This also means: So I must bother other people. If I can't play the leading role, I won't play any more.

(Results of Intelligence Test: generally above average; in advance of her age. Very good comprehension. Definitions slightly deficient. Factual information: somewhat retarded; but good in practical things. Seems to be occupied with household activities. Memory slightly below average.)

Dr. A.: It would be very important for such a child to be placed in some kind of recreation home which I consider, and require, as an indispensable addition to our Consultation Center. Such a home would have to be run by highly trained teachers and psychologists. The object would be to change the child's false style of life, with the help of parents and teachers. It is impossible to change the child in ten minutes. It would be especially beneficial for the child not to be left entirely to her mother, that someone else steps in and shows her the possibilities for making herself significant in a useful way.

(To the mother): We would like to help you and the teacher. You know, we like the child. She knows what she wants. But perhaps she doesn't like school?

The mother: She wanted to go to the Y Street School.

Dr. A.: Why does she prefer that school?

The mother: She believes she wasn't assigned to that school because she is the worst student.

Dr. A.: How does she behave at home?

The mother: She is the youngest. The older children tease her. I have had fourteen children. . . .

Dr. A.: I congratulate you.

The mother: One more mouth to feed doesn't mean anything. The older children are jealous of her and don't like her.

Dr. A.: Does she have any friends?

The mother: Oh yes, of course.

Dr. A.: We have confidence in this child. We think she is a capable girl. She always wants to be the leader, doesn't she?

The mother: She complains a lot that the teacher doesn't call on her in class. At home she is very sweet; she helps me a lot.

Dr. A.: What kind of upbringing has she had? Was it strict?

The mother: You have to be strict with all of them.

Dr. A.: I believe that if one explained things to this child, that would work, too.

The mother: You never get anywhere without punishing them.

Dr. A.: I was thinking that we could find someone around here who understands the child, who would take walks with her, who would give her better ideas—in short, if she had some company—it would be good for her. If you are willing, I could send one of my students.

The mother: She has already been to the children's play group.

Dr. A.: I think it would be better if she were under the young lady's influence outside of school. She could learn something useful from her.

The mother: I believe I've given my other children a good up-bringing, and I think I can manage to raise this one, too.

Dr. A.: This little one would like to be the biggest. Do you remember the story of Joseph? With the child making so much trouble at school as she is right now, there is nothing to be gained from punishing her. You should always be friendly. If you are willing, we will send the young lady to you.

The mother: The things she does at school are just her way of joking. You have higher-class children there, too, and they are very touchy.

Dr. A. (after the mother's departure): You can see her resistance to let anyone interfere. For the time being, we'll just have to draw back.

(To the child): What a grown-up girl! I had the idea you were much smaller. You probably always want to appear bigger than you are—you'd like to stand on your toes so that everybody would notice you. The youngest child in a family often has this feeling: he wants to be noticed. You are a good student, a capable girl. And they tell me you are an intelligent child. Don't you think you could be one of the best in your class because of what you know? If you succeeded in that, you would also get what you really want. Then everybody would esteem you and like you. Don't you want to try it? We all want to help you so you can please your teacher. Then everybody would respect you. Do you think you can do it?

The child remains silent throughout the entire conversation.

Dr. A.: You could become one of the best students. What do you say to that? Wouldn't that be nice? You wouldn't have to go on fighting. That would be nicer. You must always remember to tell yourself: "I don't have to be in the front of things all the time, and have everybody notice me. It is much nicer to do good work so that in the end people will esteem me, and like me; it doesn't have to be right away, either." How many pupils are there in your class?

The child: Thirty-two.

Dr. A.: The teacher can't do the same thing with all the others that she is doing with you. Do you want to help her a little? I have to tell you that it isn't easy, but I think you can do it.

Come back in a month. In the meantime, I'll find out whether you have succeeded, or whether you persist in being the center of attention in your class.

The child: (no reply).

Dr. A. (after having dismissed the child): Basically, she's a sensitive girl: it would have been quite easy to make her cry. Obviously, we'll have to wait and see what happpens. I want to point out something to you. I have the impression that it is a good idea to have a child appear in front of a group of people. For the child this signifies that her difficulties are not a private matter, since strangers are also interested in them. It may be that her social sense is better awakened in this way. I always tell them: "I will find out how you're doing." This is not a threat. What I want to have the child understand is the certainty that someone is waiting to see the results. In our method there is an artistic aspect which cannot be understood scientifically. If I touch the right spot, the child will certainly understand me; and this, "being in a community" is a major factor. There may also be objections; for instance, that it may make a child conceited if he notices the attention he is attracting; or that it may frighten the child. This can be remedied by the way in which one speaks to the child. It seems to be the spirit of our time to formulate objections and then do nothing.

* 5 *

The Alleged Crises of Puberty

Complaints have been made about a girl, fourteen years old, who reportedly started a number of sexual relations, who disappeared from home for ten days, and who was found near her parents' house.

Background: a poor family with three children. The oldest child, a boy, was sick for a long time. He is now earning his living and gives all his money to his mother, who therefore appreciates him most. Not only did he need the mother's care, but the father was also continuously sick, and could work for only short periods of time. It is easy to see that this girl could not have enjoyed any special attentions under these trying circumstances. A third child was born later, also a girl. At this time the father and the son were improving in health, which made it possible for the mother to give more time to the youngest child. This was an especially unfavorable situation for the middle child. Her mother had no time to give to her, and she felt she was being neglected. She was growing up as a *detested* child, lacking the warmth of mother love. Actually, a certain balance was established; but the girl lived under the impression that she was at a disadvantage with respect to her brother and sister. The father very definitely stood for authority; and the children willingly obeyed him, although he was strict. We could expect that this girl who developed like a hated child, would be hopeless since she did not experience the same warm atmosphere as the others. Such a child experiences what we have described every minute of her life; her life style is characterized by it.

A happy circumstance developed: the child entered the class of a teacher whom she likes very much. She blossomed out and became one of the best students in the class. It was predicted that she would go far. Then, when she was fourteen, she had to move on to high school, and so *change school*. The trouble begins again. The new teacher does not understand the child's personality and treats her harshly. Now we must remember that this child's only strength came from the admiration she had enjoyed at school. The fact that the teacher treats her without affection is enough to set off her self-doubts. She cannot answer when called upon, and she receives bad grades. She is in the trap which had already been prepared before. We can predict that sooner or later this *bad beginning* will take its toll. She will make progress only if she receives affection and praise.

She begins to play hooky. The teacher investigates and discovers that she is hanging around with boys. It is decided to expel her from school. This is the worst thing that could be done to her. Her success at school is over, she feels neglected at home. What is left for her? The art of Individual Psychology consists in identifying oneself with the situation in which this girl finds herself. We can pose the problem as follows: What would I do if I were a girl fourteen years old who wanted to be appreciated, but found no appreciation at home? There is only one way: to seek this appreciation from the other sex. She did this intelligently, although in contradiction to common sense. Knowing that this girl is intelligent, we can predict what will happen now: she will not get from the other sex the appreciation she is looking for. Fleeting affairs like this represent only an apparent success. Anyone who has a certain amount of experience in observing sexual relationships knows that relations like this, which are so easily established, must end in failure. She sees herself as the object, the plaything of the men. If we continue to identify ourselves with this situation, what is there to be done now? There is only suicide. She receives no recognition from anywhere. There are a few letters announcing her suicide. And it might have happened if a fortunate circumstance had not kept her from it. The fact that she did not carry out her plan should not be considered as evidence of cowardice. It is rather the act of suicide itself which represents cowardice. A discouraged person commits suicide in a burst of anger.

Something else stopped her: the relatively favorable situation of the family. Her parents were fair-minded people. She knew this, and she also knew that they would forgive her under any circumstances. The way back to the paternal home was left open to her, and she could find some kind of appreciation there. Thus we could have told her mother: "Take a walk around your house: there is where you will find your daughter." Because she *had* to take this course. And in fact the mother did find her one day, and brought her back home. The mother then turned to a counselling center.

This girl who is so hungry for appreciation must be given a chance to find appreciation. We must find out in what area the child received her best training for useful activity. It turns out to be *school*. Individual Psychology states: If such a child receives the impression of a lack of affection, she develops a strong feeling of inferiority, along with all the consequences of an inadequate preparation for society. Her interest in the family is very small, and her lack of courage is easy to see. If she had not had a strong feeling of inferiority she would have told herself: "The teacher doesn't understand me. Maybe I should try harder." She held on to her idea of gaining recognition. It seemd to her that she succeeded in this through her sexual adventures.

At this point I would like to point out something about the psy-

4

chology of puberty. It is commonly regarded as though the devil has taken possession. All evils are attributed to the sexual glands. This is a ridiculous argument. The sexual glands have been active since birth, and even before birth. Puberty is characterized by other factors: more freedom, more possibilities, and a greater attraction for the other sex. Children are powerfully stimulated by the urge to *prove* that they are no longer children. In proving it they often go too far. The girl strives for recognition, and believes she can only find it in this area. Puberty is not a disease; it only shows what had been there before. Nothing changes; the girl is as she was before. Had she really changed, we could not predict anything. She simply abandoned a road which seemed blocked for her. Nothing else happened. It is important to note that people are not led into error by facts but simply by their misinterpretation of the real facts. Those who believe that human psychic life is based on causality are mistaken. This girl creates a cause: withheld affection suddenly becomes a cause. If she is cured, there is no longer any cause. Not content with elevating withheld affection to the rank of a cause, she makes it responsible for consequences which she herself has produced. It was not absolutely indispensable that she seek elsewhere for the affection she did not get from her teacher. That was her error. We are right when we refuse to believe in the effect of inborn drives. We take into account the errors of human psychic life. It is not the facts which count, but the opinion we have of them. Individual Psychology has taken the decisive step forward which involves seeking out the possibilities of error and reducing them to a minimum by treatment. The conclusions of two human beings may be fundamentally different. We cannot ignore that facts are misunderstood and misinterpreted by a great many people.

This girl must be given the chance to prove that she is capable of doing what seemed to be ruled out for her; namely, becoming a good student. Here again, new difficulties arise: her background, and the fact that she was expelled from school. I don't see why children should be excluded from school. It only means that the teacher is not capable of solving the problem of this pupil. The child-guidance centers have helped in this area. In schools which have such child-guidance centers, students are not expelled, and pupils do not have to repeat a year of school. If there is such a case and we cannot keep the student in school, we must see what can be done. I do not see why such a child would constitute a menace for another school. We must not forget what a heavy burden the stigma of expulsion imposes on a child. Perhaps it would be simpler to consult someone competent. Perhaps the child could be entrusted to a teacher who knows what he can do with her. Everything must be done to give the girl a chance to repeat her past success at school, then the "problem of puberty" will also pass.

* 6 *

The Only Child

The teacher: The child is in the fourth grade. There are both boys and girls in the class. I have had this child for two years. The first year and the second year, he changed teachers. He is an only child. The father and mother both work. The boy stays with his grandmother, and does not obey her. He does whatever he wants to. The boy's hearing is impaired, he has a good memory for figures, and a certain critical sense. His penmanship is deplorable.

Last year he was very talkative, very disorderly, and bothered the other boys and girls. He remained indifferent to exhortations and punishments. When I tried to talk to him, he would cry and promise to be better, but very soon he started all over again.

This year it is the same. He uses his inkwell as a spittoon, and breaks all the inkwell tops. I have tried kindness and severity both. I have pretended not to notice, and not to attach importance to his tricks. Nothing works. He always tried to attract attention in one way or another.

The children had set aside some money, at school, for a big outing. He had brought only two schillings. During the recess the other children reported that K had sixteen schillings. I asked him to give me the money, and asked where he had gotten it. He replied, "That's from my savings bank." I told him his mother could get the money at the principal's office, because in view of his carelessness it was better not to risk his losing it on the way home. The mother did not appear. I knew very well that the child had not told his parents about the money, since they are very nice people and often ask how the boy is getting on at school. Finally I made an official request that the mother come to the school. It now came out that the boy had stolen the twenty schillings. The mother was very upset about this and said she remembered several occasions when small sums of money had disappeared at home. I have often noticed this at school too. When the child is faced with proof that he has lied, he looks so blankly that one has the impression he is mentally retarded.

He was present when his mother broke into tears in the principal's office. He was gently reprimanded. Then he was sent back to his class, where he played tricks and amused all the pupils. The mother was frightened and said her husband would kill the boy. We advised her to say nothing to her husband for the time being. The next day the father came to the school. The mother had told him everything, and he had not punished the child.

The latter put the blame on an older boy who, so he claimed, had talked him into stealing. This boy does not go to any school. Supposedly he is enrolled at the High School D.

Dr. A.: We hear a few details clearly, and in all of them—the same refrain. The boy is disorderly. Probably there is always someone behind him who puts things in order. At school he works slowly. His style of life is that of a pampered child. Other facts seem to indicate the same. He always wants someone to pay attention to him. In school he wants to make himself conspicuous. It would be especially useful to know just when he showed his fault (stealing) most. We must draw our own conclusions.

For the past two years the mother is not at home. The child stays with his grandmother, and seems to be dissatisfied there. He feels deprived, he lacks many things his mother gave him. We see in him the trend to enrich himself. Stealing is a compensation to replace what he has lost. We must also consider the boy's statement that an older boy instigated him. There is no delinquent or criminal who does not try to excuse himself, who does not seek a justification which will make his misdeeds look less serious. This shows us that the boy knows very well that he strayed from the path of society, of social feeling. He stole because he wanted to make himself look bigger. He could find no other way. He was used to his mother's company, and then he found himself in a more difficult situation. His grandmother does not have the same attitude toward him that his mother had. She is stricter. He fights the older woman. Tension develops between them. Such a child, who has the habit of leaning on others, feels he is in a trap. His style of life is already fixed, he always wants someone who will pay attention to him. He no longer gets this at home. It was at this point, I imagine, that he started to steal. What might have prevented him from stealing? If in school he had a position where he was appreciated. But this is particularly difficult for spoiled children. If such a child decides he wants to have everything, just as he did when he was with his mother, he is acting intelligently, and he is not feeble-minded.

He is now exposed before the teacher. He is used to being treated with kid gloves. The father has been calmed down, and the boy believes that consequently everything has been put back in order. He will respond to every privation and every frustration with a new attempt at enriching himself. I do believe that he began stealing only two years ago. It must go farther back into his past. What did he do with the missing two schillings? I would say he bought some candy. (The teacher: He bought a sausage.) How did he think up the idea that another boy urged him on? How did he know that an older boy can lead another one astray? It would be a good idea to ask the mother whether she didn't put him on guard by telling him, "Don't have anything to do with that boy. He might lead you astray." Or perhaps there really was an older boy who won his sympathy. If he had the money with him for quite a while, he must have had some other purpose. Perhaps he wanted to have something to fall back on. We should ask his mother about this. We also have to look for other manifestations, manifestations which we usually find in pampered children. Perhaps he is fearful, and doesn't want to be alone. If so, we can understand why he took up with an older boy. This is not necessarily the case, but we can draw our own conclusions. Also, he may cry out at night. The mother could also tell us whether the child had previously evinced a tendency to steal.

We shall also notice that he does not take much interest in others, and that his way of treating them is not the right one. He is incapable of making friends. When he plays with others he always wants to be the captain. He has a tendency to associate with children younger or older than himself. In only children one often finds a predilection for older persons, since these children have always lived among older people. We must agree on how we can influence the mother. We should also see to it that the boy makes progress at school, and we must stimulate his courage. He must be given the hope of playing an important role at school, of gaining attention. I advise you to acquire a skill in recognizing what I call the radius of action. In problem children this radius of action is always narrowed. We must try to enlarge it. This is possible only when he has more courage, when he believes that he, too, can achieve something. This would give him the chance to change his circle of action completely. In the tight corner where he is now, nothing is left to him but to enrich himself secretly and to prevent by lying, loss of status and esteem.

The teacher: He is bad only in penmanship and spelling, otherwise he is well-liked in school, the children like him and he is certainly not rejected. He is not disliked in class. He has never failed a grade. He is a slow student, but he learns rather well.

Dr. A.: We are trying to find out why he is not satisfied at school. One of the main reasons must be that he always wants to be the center of attention. Such a child tries to get there by clowning, or else by treating others with kindness. He is always concerned with his own person. This boy tries to get everything he wants in a sly way. He is not like those who play "wild" to achieve something. He wants to get everything that seems desirable to him by using his charm. He has been conditioned for this by the attitude of his mother, who has always pampered him.

Another teacher: I had a student who also stole. I caught him stealing half a schilling from another child. He declared that other children had everything, his father never gave him anything because he was poor. He wanted to have everything, like the other children. I gave him some change so he too could buy something. I did this several times, and from that moment on I have never heard of his stealing again.

Dr. A.: We don't have any rules for improving a child. Our treatment has a different effect on each child. The same measure can't be applied all the time. Aside from the small change this child received a feeling of belonging which has a much more important effect. I wouldn't be surprised if someone told me: "I beat him, and from then on he didn't steal any more." These things are too complex to be evaluated all at once. What we try to do above all, is to understand the child. This particular child lives with the idea that he has a right to everything—immediately and with no effort. This is a mistake and we want to explain this to the child so that he can correct it.

The teacher: The child's family situation is good.

Dr. A.: Do you generally find at your school that the poorer children are in the slower groups, while those whose parents are better off are in groups where the work is faster?

The teacher replies in the affirmative.

Dr. A.: If you look hard enough you will not find a single man who has not stolen something at some time in his life: some fruit, candy, trifles, etc. In my own work I have found that this is almost always true.

Dr. A. (to the parents): I would like to talk to your boy. It is possible to get rid of his bad habits. In many ways he seems to be a peculiar child. Haven't you found that he is looking for affection? He is always finding something so that he can be with you? He is always waiting for someone to do something for him. Does he make trouble at meal-time?

(The mother says that he used to be difficult about eating, but that during the past year he has been eating properly.)

Dr. A.: Was he sick? Did he wet the bed?

The mother: He has always looked sickly, and he has always had trouble with his stomach.

Dr. A.: Was he afraid? Afraid of staying alone? Did he go to kindergarten? What role does he play? *Does he have friends?*

The father: We don't know about that. He wasn't afraid. But he asks stupid questions. He'll say, "Mother, what's that?" He knows very well what it is. He just wants to bother his mother.

Dr. A.: How does he do his homework? Does he do them alone, or does he need help?

The father: If somebody is standing over him, he does it very well. He doesn't like the old German script very much; he prefers Roman letters. He prefers the company of grown-ups, they are more friendly to him.

Dr. A.: Does he know how to swim? Does he have nightmares? Is he superstitious? Does he like gymnastics?

The father: He has a great respect for swimming. But he was frightened once, and since then he doesn't want to swim any more. He is quite fond of gymnastics. Last year he took gymnastics regularly. He doesn't have nightmares, and he is not fearful. He is a little afraid of me because I am very nervous.

Dr. A.: Be gentle with him, and take walks with him when your wife isn't along so that he will form a friendship with you and will do what you want out of love and friendship, and not out of fear.

Dr. A.: Doesn't he have trouble with penmanship and spelling? Have you investigated to see whether he isn't left-handed? Perhaps he was born left-handed.

(The parents don't know whether he is left-handed. It seems that the mother is left-handed.)

The mother complains once again that her son refused to give the name of the boy who talked him into stealing, and that he gave a fictitious name.

Dr. A.: Doesn't he go to visit other children? How is he about dressing himself, washing up, and combing his hair?

The father: He had a friend he used to play with, but he died.

The mother: When he is dressing, I have to keep him at it until he is ready.

Dr. A.: It isn't necessary to keep after him. The important thing is to make him independent, gradually and very gently. If you want me to, I will try to influence him. Does he like to go to school? Does he say what he wants to do later on? Is he conceited? What position does he sleep in? Does he bite his fingernails? Does he put his fingers in his nose?

(The parents state that he is very conceited; that he would like to become a carpenter; that he used to bite his nails; that otherwise they have not noticed anything unusual about him. He goes to school willingly.)

Dr. A.: Make him more independent so that he will take even more interest in school and will be able to make a place for himself there. That will keep him out of the kind of trouble he has been in. Don't threaten him, and don't talk to him about this matter any more. It is very interesting to discover that this boy, who has had so much stomach trouble, buys things like sausages. Don't reproach him any more, and try to make him independent.

Dr. A.: We do not have here a pure image of a pampered child. The image is distorted by the fact that the boy has been reared with a view toward freedom. There is a great difference between a child who is constantly watched over, and one who is used to being alone.

(In the meantime the boy has come in, and Dr. Adler speaks to him):

What do you want to do later on in life?

The child: I want to become a carpenter.

Dr. A.: What will you do when you are a carpenter?

The child: Use a plane.

Dr. A.: How many friends do you have?

The child: Three.

Dr. A.: What do they do?

The child: *They steal.*

Dr. A.: I would tell them, "What will become of you if you do these things?" Do you obey willingly?

The child: No.

Dr. A.: Why then do you do what these boys tell you? I have the idea that you thought nobody would notice you had stolen something, and that you could buy something with the money. Are you afraid? You are brave, and you must also be brave at school. You are already a big boy. You should be doing everything yourself. You know how to dress yourself and wash yourself. Do you also do it, or does your mother have to help you? You want to give her more work to do. But you already know how to do everything yourself, so don't wait until your mother helps you. How are you coming along with your penmanship? Do some extra work in it and things will go better.

(The child is also left-handed.)

Don't believe such nonsense that others led you astray. You mustn't let yourself be led astray. Come back in a month and then you can tell me if you are doing everything yourself, if you are trying hard in penmanship, and if you are letting others lead you along. (He dismisses the child.)

Left-handed children receive the impression that they are less capable of solving problems than others. They try to work with the right hand; and when they see that it doesn't go well, they imagine that things will always go badly with them. It is possible to diagnose a left-handedness on the basis of many symptoms. When a child has trouble reading, writing, etc., it indicates that he may be left-handed. In most cases the left half of the face is better developed than the right. Many left-handed children present difficulties. A large number of them give up hope of making progress; their handwriting will be bad for the rest of their lives. Others, on the contrary, make a special effort and learn to write very well, just as if they were right-handed. These are the ones who have overcome their left-handedness and in doing so have acquired a great aptitude. They often become artists, etc. If you see someone with fine penmanship which he has achieved with his right hand, you should remember that he might have been left-handed. In Vienna you will find about thirty-five to fifty per cent left-handed persons. They may not know it, but they have felt it. You will find a very large number of left-handed persons among the best and the worst of men; among problem people— from artists to delinquent children.

In this particular case the boy is sickly, an only child, pampered by his mother, and treated harshly by his father—which prompts him even more to take refuge with his mother. The father should come to an agreement with her concerning the child's upbringing. Now a new situation has arisen, for which the child was not prepared. He has gone to live with his grandmother, and does not get along with her; she wants her peace and quiet. At school he is making good progress, and yet he breaks out of the norm. He is making progress because he is able to make progress there. He is looking for compensation; he disturbs the teacher and makes the children laugh. When that isn't enough, he wants to steal. Let us assume that he has been instigated by another boy. This fitted his purpose. He didn't let himself be led along in the matter of practicing his penmanship. He has the impression that he is not being treated as warmly as he was used to being treated in the past. He may be in a more favorable situation now, but he is not hopeful. Perhaps previously he was not received so kindly at school as he is now. One should think in terms of encouraging him. He should not be pressured; you must have patience with him. Perhaps he should be told: "I can see that everything will be all right. I know that you are going to be one of the best students again." He has always wanted the teacher to pay attention to him. If he should once again behave badly, I would tell him in a humorous way: "It isn't even worth your trouble. We are all interested in you." A remark of this kind might impress him. How it should be made depends upon the individual personality. I would perhaps do it in such a "slightly humorous" way.

* 7 *

The Discouraged Youngest Child

"Emil is fourteen years old."

This is the age of puberty. We know that this "problem" is regarded in different ways by various authors. Some of them have supposed that at this age a child is, as it were, possessed by the devil, or perhaps under the influence of an internal poison. But today we know that nothing can manifest itself without having existed previously in a latent form. The major factor is that during puberty the child has an urge to demonstrate that he is an adult and no longer a child. If I try to prove that I am no longer a child, I will always go too far. I will make exaggerated movements, and I will try to imitate adults in every respect. The supposition of psychologists (who are not physicians) which holds that the sexual glands do not develop until puberty, must be rejected.

"He is the youngest of six children. The other five range in age from seventeen to twenty-six. At primary school he was always among the best students; but since he has entered secondary school he has dropped behind, and is threatened with expulsion from school.

This is the typical victorious striving of the youngest as long as he is in a favorable situation. But if the situation changes then we see that he has not been adequately prepared. He can adapt only if he is one of the leaders.

"He had to take a year of school over again, and since then he has progressed only with great difficulty.

The trouble no doubt began earlier, when he entered secondary school. He cannot cope with this new situation. Secondary School has its own requirements. The teachers are new to him. They do not yet know this former prince, and do not treat him with enough affection. He is offended and relegated to the background. In primary school things were easy for him, and he was well thought of. Now he is running into difficulties, and he no longer makes progress.

"He says he no longer likes school because it gives him more pain than pleasure."

Although expressed differently, this means what we have just said:

he feels at ease only when he gets satisfaction, and when he can be the leader.

"Secondary school seems especially detestable to him since one of his former schoolmates from primary school, who didn't do particularly well there, has managed not to repeat a year of school and is now a year ahead of him."

The youngest child cannot bear it when someone gets ahead of him. He has travelled a long way in order to surpass the others, and he has fought against many difficulties.

"He complains of the bad treatment he has to undergo at school, and he puts most of the blame for this on his class teacher, who (he says) makes life hard for him through his malice."

Thus if one merely ceases to pamper him, he immediately shows his bad temper.

"The mother says that as soon as he entered secondary school he changed in every respect, to his disadvantage."

The basic question which we often pose is the following: In what situations has he given grounds for complaint, and at what particular times did his faults appear? Secondary school may be considered as a test. The fact that he has completely changed since he entered secondary school indicates that he was not well prepared for this situation. The second question is: Why was this boy inadequately prepared? We know he is the youngest child, and that the youngest child is usually pampered. Therefore, in our investigation we should try to ascertain whether he is in fact a pampered child.

"He is nervous and irritable. . . ."

Like someone who feels annoyed and in a situation which oppresses him.

". . . very excitable, and in general not obedient."

We can understand why his behavior is so bad at home. So long as an individual is having some success and things are going well, the repercussions will be felt in other areas. If this boy were succeeding at school the fact would be noticeable at home. We can compare his behavior to that of a subordinate employee who has trouble on his job, where he is abused and criticized, and who when he goes home at night usually quarrels with his wife and children. This is the usual case. The child would like to be in the top position—at least at home. And this is expressed by the fact that he is disobedient.

"According to his mother he is a good boy and knows how to win over his family with his good nature and his endearments."

You will often find spoiled children who are very skillful at winning over others and gaining their affection. One frequently has the impression of a special kind of charm on their part.

"When he sees that his mother is crying or suffering, he will do anything for her."

Here he is the one who gives, since he has already achieved his goal: namely, to tyrannize, and to dominate his mother. Thus, he can afford to demonstrate his affection. Moreover, this is an intelligent way to act. If he behaved callously he would perhaps be put in a boarding school so that his family would not have to suffer from his callousness, in addition to his poor school work, and he would have lost the game. We can see that this child still has hope. If he did not have hope, he would not show his kindness and his feeling. It must be his intention to keep his mother's favor and gain support from her. We shall not consider his kindness as a virtue but rather as a trick to avoid tightening the strings to the breaking point.

"The father has been away from the home for three years."

It may have been this circumstance which brought about the change in his attitude toward school. The father's departure may have coincided with the period of preparation for entering secondary school; and this departure may have left a deep impression on the child. Perhaps he wanted to leave with his father. Perhaps this is when the new situation began. The father, who loved him but who also put limits on him, is now absent. Now the child wants to play at being "a big shot."

"In the mother's opinion the firm hand is missing."

This is a valuable piece of information with regard to the mother's style of life. She evidently has the convicttion that in this situation a woman is much too weak, and that only a man could get results. If at this point I would maintain that the mother shows inferiority feeling with this remark, many people would not understand me. Yet when she says "The boy lacks a firm hand" she is also saying: "I am too weak. I can not succeed." She can do nothing beyond showing her suffering.

"She maintains that she cannot handle the boy.

"For the past six months he has been sleeping in his mother's room."

Perhaps he has tried for this and achieved it. Or it may be that the mother felt the need for his presence. In any case this shows an attachment which is strong but excessive, if we consider that the boy is already fourteen years old.

"He always has to be compelled to eat."

A common symptom in pampered children is that they make trouble about eating.

"In general he does not follow the orders that are given to him. He often stays in bed until nine o'clock and is late to school."

The reason for this is that he feels a distance between himself and school. If a child is late for school it usually indicates that he is on bad terms with school.

"In such cases he does not eat breakfast; and he often brings his lunch home with him."

Here we have the mother's sensitive point. The child has detected it very accurately, and is torturing her with it. The mother exaggerated the importance of food, and showed this sensitive spot too. She overestimated it, thereby revealing it clearly to the boy; now he holds on to it.

"According to his mother he does not usually lie; only sometimes where money is concerned."

The mother is not expressing a very clear opinion here, since it is nonetheless a question of lying.

"His ambition seems to express itself in other areas."

This confirms what I thought I had detected in an earlier place. He would like to be the leader somewhere. He has not given up hope, and is looking around how to accomplish this.

"He is first soloist in the choir at a big temple."

Thus we see that he has managed to be a leader. Now the question arises: Why isn't he satisfied with this? (We should note that he has a brother who is an excellent singer and gives concerts.) It is apparent that it is not enough for him to have become first soloist in the choir. His ambition is not quite satisfied. Perhaps he would like to rise still higher. He should be given an opportunity in other areas as well. Perhaps then he would behave properly at school. He has not lost all hope; he has not given up the race. But what could we expect from him if he lost his courage completely? He might either commit a crime or become neurotic. If we wanted to go more deeply into this question on the basis of the information we have at present, we would be in a relatively difficult situation. We do not find any other symptoms of insecurity. We do not find that he is aggressive; hence it is more likely that he will become neurotic. If he were active, if he also had a tendency to harm others, to attack them, we could suppose that he might pursue a career of crime. The fact that he lies where money is concerned tells us too little. We must rather assume that he will become a neurotic if he loses hope.

"For some time he has been especially skilled in riding bicycles."

The youngest child! The fact that he is expert with a bicycle is grounds for believing that he may participate in bicycle races later on.

"Right now his greatest desire is to own a bicycle. According to his mother he spends his money too freely."

If this were confirmed one might think of the possibility that the boy would be capable of stealing if he were to lose hope.

"He has a fairly large amount of money at his disposal."

This comment is probably exaggerated.

"He has some friends who go to *another school,* but his mother doesn't like them."

It is interesting to note that he does not seek his friends in the place where he is experiencing his failures, but rather seeks friends from a period when he was still on top.

"He was happy during a visit to his father, in England."

With his father his behavior must certainly have been very amiable and polite, since he was in a pleasant situation and was no longer burdened with school.

"This was probably because he didn't have to go to school."

"Recently he appears to be less sloppy."

(Treatment by Dr. V.)

Sloppiness is a sign of a spoiled child.

"An investigation made by the school indicates that the entire family is probably responsible for the child's carelessness."

"They all stay in bed until noon."

I would like to make an observation which seems to me a very important one. In our age, when the necessity for hard work by the father (and, in most cases, by the mother too) means that there are very few opportunities for bringing the family close together, it seems to me that it is particularly important for the child's later life that the whole family be together for breakfast at seven o'clock in the morning (taking our school schedules into account). You will find that where this is not done, numerous troubles arise in the family. The roots for correct social development will always be missing in families who have not trained, from the beginning, how to behave together at the table. This is the place for good humor and gaiety, for exchanging ideas, and for open discussion—but not for scolding or discussing bad grades, etc. That should be postponed to another time. It is difficult to overestimate the advantage of having the family together for breakfast. I have been emphasizing this advice for twenty years. Often the reaction is an incredulous smile, and many refuse to do it. I can state, however, that there are certain faults that I have found only in cases where this habit was not established. It is quite natural that a person who stays in bed all morning cannot go to sleep at night. Natural fatigue does not come then. When we hear complaints about children who stay away from home and spend their evenings in a bar or a movie, we can blame it on the above circumstance. By this means, so easy to employ, a lot of trouble could be avoided.

"According to the teacher the whole family lies. And a certain degree of caution in gathering information would seem to be indicated, especially since the mother apparently does not tell the truth, owing to her boasting. . . ."

If we consider what has transpired so far, we won't be able to say that the mother did much boasting. It is an incontestable fact that the boy is intelligent and has a fine voice. This probably means a lot to the mother; but I would not interpret what she says as boasting.

"Most teachers agree that the boy is a liar, inattentive, lazy, and sly."

This is harsh. Even if we admit that it is accurate, it is still a harsh criticism. The boy seems to feel that all his teachers are his enemies. These peculiarities are hostile manifestations corresponding to a permanent battle.

"But they are all convinced that the boy is not stupid, and that he could meet the school's requirements if he were in a better situation. Right now he is not meeting them."

As soon as this boy, who always wants to be the leader, encounters a difficult situation he can no longer meet the school's requirements.

We shall find here the character traits of the fighter opposing a superior force.

"He does inadequate work mostly in four subjects: mathematics, history, geography, and religion."

It is surprising that he does not do well in religion; but it may be that he does not get along with the teacher. It is interesting to note how far his work at school has fallen off. As for mathematics, you will usually find that pampered children have difficulties with this subject. It is also possible that he battles with this teacher, too.

The Intelligence Test Reveals Average Intelligence

We are convinced that the boy is intelligent. Such being the case, we ask ourselves what should be done. The therapy follows automatically from what has been said above. We must find someone who can win this child over; someone who will also encourage him and develop his interest in his schoolmates and in his subjects. This person could talk frankly to him and help him understand what up to now he has grasped only vaguely. If this is done the child will reduce his wrong attitudes to a minimum. One could tell him that everybody has difficulties and that one must be strong in the face of these difficulties. But only a person in whom the boy has confidence could succeed there. It is likely that a man would do better because the boy will regard women in the same way as he does his mother; and we know that he behaves very differently toward his father, his attitude having been aggravated beginning with the moment when his father could no longer give him his attention. An older brother might gain his confidence, if he understands the entire situation, and all its correlations. He should, without criticizing him, propose that he start a new life and forget the past entirely. He should make him understand his secret desire to become a singer. He should convince him that he lost interest in school because he believed that the only way he could play an important role was as a singer. The older brother should also ask the teachers to give the boy a certain respite; because even if the brother managed to straighten the boy out, the results would be bad if he got a bad grade from school. The poor school work he is doing at the present time can be attributed to his feeling of antagonism against the school.

* 8 *

Feeble-Minded, or Problem Child?

It is very important for us that we establish a clear picture of a particular case even before seeing the mother or the child. I shall read to you this case history, and you will see how I endeavor to draw conclusions from every bit of information.

"When B entered kindergarten, he was the most neglected and physically and mentally retarded child that one could imagine."

We can deduce from this that no one gave him any attention. It is essential to mental development that a child be closely associated with someone so that he can exercise his mind.

"He was undernourished, unkempt, poorly clothed, and had no shoes, although it was almost winter."

This child apparently came from a very poor family, a bad situation.

"Also, he was backward mentally, and could scarcely talk." A child can develop his use of language only in a social relationship. If this relationship is lacking, he cannot develop his speech. We should also ask ourselves whether the child is not perhaps feebleminded. This is only a hypothesis, and we should be cautious in our further investigations, because if we put forth such a diagnosis, the fate of the child will be sealed. To call a child feeble-minded when in fact he is not, is an unpardonable mistake.

"When spoken to, he would hide and begin to cry and writhe about."

If someone tries to make contact with him, he blocks it. He would seem to belong to the third category of children: those who are unwanted, illegitimate, or crippled. It is plain that he has a hostile attitude toward those around him.

"He was very cowardly . . ."

A human being has courage only when he feels that he belongs.

"He attacked the other children, but was always afraid of being attacked by them."

"He required help at mealtime, and always waited for someone to feed him."

This bit of information must be taken with a grain of salt. It is usually pampered children who have difficulties with eating. But it is possible that he expects a hostile attitude even on this occasion.

Indeed, it is possible that an unwanted child is fed, just in order to get rid of him more quickly. As a result, he doesn't learn to eat.

"But he often refused food, although he was hungry."

The child behaves as though he were in enemy territory. But we must look closely to see whether he doesn't show signs of being feeble-minded.

"It was only after making a scene (which, incidentally, would be totally ignored by those around him) , that he would calm down and eat—and then he would eat ravenously."

Hence it turns out that he ate quite well after all.

"He is a legitimate child. He was very slow in learning to walk and to talk; and up to the present has not learned to speak correctly."

We can understand his problem as regards talking. But what about his walking? We can observe that children who receive attention have fewer difficulties with learning to walk. We must consider organic defects. Perhaps the child suffered from rickets, and perhaps his teething was delayed, which is part of the same illness.

"He made a great deal of trouble . . ."

But he can make trouble only if there is someone around him. A surprising comment. Perhaps his neglected condition is a result of his parents' despair. And perhaps there was someone in the family who took care of him: perhaps a grandmother, an aunt, or an older sister who was at his disposal to a certain extent. We can draw our own conclusions and understand why he behaved as he did in kindergarten. If our theory is not confirmed, we will willingly correct it.

". . . and rebelled at the least provocation."

It is probable that his family did not treat him with any real harshness. To resist is a way of rebelling; and when those around him are particularly strong, a child does not rebel. Perhaps at some previous time he was in a milieu where he was given a certain amount of affection, and then this ceased to be the case. We must remember this in order to continue our investigation.

"He kicked, rolled on the floor, screamed, and struck at everything that came near him."

This also seems to indicate that his environment changed for the worse. A change of his situation must have taken place. Our two suppositions are correct: after having been pampered at first, he was subsequently neglected. And this made him wild and hostile.

"He wets his bed constantly."

This indicates that he wants to make trouble for someone and tried to get attention by being bad.

"And he bites his fingernails."

You will almost always find this habit in stubborn children. They are constantly being told not to bite their nails, and it is by persisting in it that they show their opposition.

"He was so greedy at mealtime that occasionally, when the children were having their lunch, he would take something away from another child."

He does not have much social feeling, and this becomes evident at this point.

"He suffered badly from rickets, and was very backward mentally."

This is a confirmation.

"He was not sociable, and he did not get along with anyone."

This is true for the pampered child as well as for the hated child.

"He tortures animals and human beings."

This can also be found in both types. They want to demonstrate their power.

"He took great pleasure in squashing flies."

You see, he proves himself strong against the weak.

"He always wanted to be first."

The opinion that originally he was a pampered child has been confirmed. His parents were perhaps in a better situation previously, and it changed. Since then he has lacked love and warmth.

"He was always giving orders. If he did not succeed he would strike his schoolmates, upset tables and chairs, throw himself on the floor, and refuse to listen to kindly approaches."

These are the character traits of a pampered child who wants always to be at the center of attention.

"Now he goes to kindergarten willingly, and he tries to see that he always has the handkerchief I gave him as a present.'"

He is now beginning to adapt—a sign which enables us to conclude that he already has a relationship with the kindergarten teacher. We observe that she has been able to win him over, and to recreate the agreeable situation in which he was pampered. He has the impression: You are in that agreeable situation which you always wanted. Now his interest for others must be awakened, which has not been accomplished yet.

"He is interested in the things that are shown to him here. He is happy if he is constantly occupied; for example, feeding a bird, watering flowers, sweeping, helping younger children to put on their shoes, etc."

Our guess that he might be feeble-minded is beginning to weaken. Apparently he is adapting, he has established contact with the kindergarten teacher, and is acting intelligently. It seems to me that there are insufficient grounds for a diagnosis of feeble-mindedness, and that it is hardly tenable any longer.

"His family situation is very pathetic. His father died of tuberculosis; his mother is an unskilled factory worker and does not pay any attention to his education."

Where is the person who pampered him? Perhaps it was his father before he died.

"She often sells the child's clothes (as she did the winter coat, shoes, and other things we gave him) and sends him back to us in rags."

Just imagine the situation of this child, who is unwanted, brought up without love, and without warmth (almost in the literal sense, since his mother sold his winter coat).

"He is the youngest child. The other children are boys aged ten, fifteen, and nineteen."

This makes us think that perhaps one of these other children gave him particular care. As for his development, we must bear in mind his position as the youngest child. If we remember that he was pampered, it is certain that, as the youngest child, he had a certain power. He had three older brothers, and wanted to be like them. He didn't want the others to have more power than he himself possessed. And he wanted to be in the lead; he wanted to get to the top.

"He cries often, but only when he is showing his opposition or when he is angry."

Crying is an especially efficient weapon. If children notice that their crying has no effect on us, they will stop. He employs tears to gain recognition.

There was a deaf-mute couple who had a boy whose speech and hearing were good. When he hurt himself, he would cry, but without making any noise. Tears would run down his cheeks, but no sound would be heard. We can understand this very well, since the boy knew that sound had no effect on his parents. One always finds the imprint of the environment.

"His favorite games are gymnastics and using building blocks."

This child is probably not so clumsy and backward as was thought.

"His favorite stories are 'Rumpelstiltskin' and 'The Sleeping Beauty.'"

To draw conclusions from such stories can be very fruitful. The first story involves cleverness which is overcome by another cleverness. The choice of "The Sleeping Beauty" strikes us as more understandable. No doubt he likes this story because in a way it expresses the hope of gaining a certain success by exceptional bravery. I feel that this matter should be explored more thoroughly in order to ascertain what elements in these stories impress children particularly. When we know this boy better, we will also understand more clearly why he prefers these two stories.

"He often day-dreams."

If this means that the child is given to fantasies, it is reminiscent of "The Sleeping Beauty," who also sleeps. Perhaps we shall find a thread which will help us to understand this child better.

"Until fairly recently he would fall asleep from sheer weakness, which made us fear that some day he would not wake up."

Perhaps this weakness was associated with the idea of "The Sleeping Beauty." I can see why a child of this kind would be more interested in sleep than other children, since he was so fond of a story like "The Sleeping Beauty."

"Apparently the child has been beaten."

The mother, probably, is not sparing with beatings.

"He feels rejected by everyone, and demands attention."

This trait is not found in the hated child who turns his back and tries to slip away. It is the spoiled child who always demands attention.

"Praise is everything to him. When you tell him, 'Come on. You're a brave boy,' his eyes shine, and for the moment all is well."

He has the personality of a pampered child. He feels at ease in this kind of situation. It is the goal of his life—of his strivings.

"Once he starts a job he sees it through to the end. And if he is praised for it, he is more than ready to start all over again."

Here is the lever which can direct this boy. In the beginning he works because it opens up a situation in which he is praised and liked. Therefore, this situation should be utilized. It should be made clear to him that he should make himself useful, without expecting immediate praise. Rather than to praise him immediately, one should tell him: "If you do it that way, it will be very good."

"He behaves like a child of two. He plays stupid or pretends to be a baby so people will caress him and pamper him."

You will often find that spoiled children or even adults behave like babies. They often talk and lisp like small children. They long for their former situation: they would like to go back to a time when they seemed to be in Paradise. It is probable that this boy was pampered during his illness. There are some critical situations in this illness where there is nothing left but to pamper the child. Hence his need to be pampered, and his striving to be praised for his efforts and to be loved. He does not know it, but this is the way he lives. Thus it is possible to achieve improvement by explaining this to him.

"He speaks very badly. He is well formed physically, but there is an occasional discharge from his ears."

It is probably inflammation of the middle ear which is not yet cured. If he has not been seriously damaged by this illness, it may very well be that he is more receptive to listening and music than other children, since his ear is probably more sensitive than the average ear. Not all children can get middle ear infection. Perhaps a new area could be opened to him because of this condition. He might be brought into close touch with society by means of instrumental music or singing in a choral group.

"He is mentally retarded, and acts like a child of three."

A boy of five who always wants to play at being a child of three and who gives the impression that he is lacking in intelligence, might lead one to believe that he is feeble-minded. But it is necessary to test him thoroughly before drawing any conclusions.

"In general he does not react except to persons he is accustomed to."

The character trait of a spoiled child.

"His positive achievements are in the physical area. Normal and rhythmic gymnastics are his favorite activities, and he does brilliantly in them."

I do not feel that I am entitled to draw any conclusions yet. We seldom hear of good work in gymnastics and rhythmic exercises on the part of a feeble-minded child. The fact that he masters systematic movements in gymnastics and achieves top results, indicates the kind of coordination which is not possessed by a feeble-minded child.

* **9** *

Misdirected Ambition: the Youngest of Five Children

A teacher has given us the following case history.

"M is nine years old and in the fourth grade. She is the *youngest* of five children. Her brothers and sisters are respectively twenty-five, twenty-three, fifteen, and fourteen years old. The oldest girl is already married and has a baby a few months old. Being the youngest child, pretty and with a pleasant disposition, M was especially pampered by her parents and her siblings as well. Her rearing and care were largely entrusted to her brothers and sisters, since the parents worked all day. The father is employed with a commercial firm and is absent from home between seven in the morning and six at night. The mother has a corset shop, and is likewise busy all day.

"When she entered school the child was unpleasantly conspicuous in her class because of her chattering, her exaggerated vivacity, her arrogant attitude, her tendency to quarrel, and her wildness. The first grade teacher often cited her as an *enfant terrible* but intelligent and, according to her mood, sometimes very industrious and sometimes very lazy.

"I have known the child only since she entered the second grade, and I cannot say she is lazy. On the contrary, she does impeccable work, is quite good in composition, has a lively imagination, expresses herself well, recites well, has good penmanship, and insists on neatness (a result of her vanity, it must be admitted). She likes to be admired. When she has done an assignment especially well, she never fails to bring her notebook up to me, even before class starts, and remark proudly: 'There! I wrote that!' She is delighted when someone praises her. She goes at her work with skill and courage. In physical education she is very skillful and brave. She taught herself to ride the bicycle and to swim. Now she wants skates so that she can learn to skate this year. Such are her good qualities.

"But her tendency to assert herself is overly strong. She constantly insists on being noticed—something quite impossible in a group of thirty children. When she isn't noticed she disturbs the classroom work by interrupting the other children without being able to control herself, although she has been reprimanded for this several times. Nor can she control her curiosity. When I point out a mistake in another student's notebook, she leaves her seat so that she, too, can see her schoolmate's error. She is particularly attracted by whatever is prohibited. Last year the principal forbade the wearing of any disguises before hallowe'en since the first grade children, who were in the adjoining classroom, might be frightened. The next day during recess M went to the rest room, and a few minutes later ran into the classroom disguised as a devil, brandishing a pitchfork, jostling the other children, and shouting. I reprimanded her and asked whether she didn't know about the prohibition against disguises. She did not answer.

"She always reacts this way when someone reprimands her. It should be noted that she can never look anyone straight in the eye. If I look at her for a certain length of time in class, she shows signs of great anxiety. At such times she will look aside in an embarrassed manner, occasionally glancing timidly in my direction to see whether I am still looking at her. However, it should be mentioned in passing that she is not dishonest. Her mother also says that she never lies.

"Her need for recognition was strikingly manifested in the following incident. Last year a school supervisor visited a singing class which followed my own class. Several times already, as a disciplinary measure, M had been expelled from this class because of her chattering and constant interrupting. This time she was admitted to the class again. Since she had not had the same training as the others she could not of course perform brilliantly. But she could not bear the thought of simply being in the ranks and doing what the others did, without making herself noticed. During recess she came up to the supervisor, who was talking with the teacher, and did a somersault, because she excells in gymnastics.

"She likes to play tricks. For example, one day she told me she had let a bird out of a cage that the landlord had put in the courtyard. She was delighted that the landlord did not find out who had played the trick. She claims she felt sorry for the bird, which was screeching. During vacation, while playing in the street, she pulled down the iron shutters of a butcher's shop located across the street from where she lives. When the butcher's wife came out and struck M, her mother emerged from her own shop and slapped the butcher's wife, which cost her a lawsuit and a fine of ten schillings.

"The mother asked me to be very severe with the child, who wears her out at home. She is stubborn, and when her mother tells her to do something, she replies: 'I'm not going to do it!' Usually, she yields only to force. If the mother had had enough money she would have put the child in the care of strangers who would have given her a proper upbringing, since the parents are too busy with their jobs to give her enough time. As for her brothers and sisters, she will have nothing to do with them, although they love her and are very affectionate with her. At school she behaves in the same way. Not a day passes when she does not hit a schoolmate or throw her to the ground for no reason at all. Twice already, two little girls have been badly hurt from being pushed against a wall or the end of a bench. On her way to school she pulls her schoolmates' hair; and at school, she threatens to beat them when school is out. Because of all these things the other children are afraid of her and don't want her in the class. If during class a girl sitting next to her asks her to sit still, she hits her, pinches her, or kicks her under the bench. So far no results have been obtained from calling the parents in for consultation. It is always the mother who comes, and she blames the father, who pampers the child. I have never been able to interview the father personally, but the mother has promised to bring him to see us today."

Dr. A.: In this detailed report on the child, the central point of her development is emphasized with great precision. This little girl shows an especially marked tendency toward misdirected self-assertion. We have been told that she is the youngest child, and that she is pampered. This seems to explain why her tendency toward self-assertion is so strong. As the youngest child she wants to surpass all the others. But together with her good work, there are so many faults that one is amazed. We can understand why the child's behavior is getting worse. She acts as though she were in a trap, and could not escape her fate. She would like to be the center of attention; but she has already behaved so badly that she encounters resistance everywhere. But she is tempted to go ever further. I would like very briefly to repeat those things in this excellent report which struck me as the child's line of movement.

She strives to be more than anybody else. At school, she has achieved only partial success; and she tried to fill in the missing part by interrupting the lesson, by her attacks, and by making trouble for her mother. We could assume that if she were at the head of her class, her conduct would change completely. She herself would not change, only her situation would be better. Her striving for recognition can not tolerate life at home, or at school; her schoolmates fight her. She would like to be victorious in this struggle. It is impossible to make this child change her course of behavior by beatings and punishment. If she no longer dared to do her damage openly, she might do it furtively. This would encourage the child to become a liar. I believe that her true motive in letting the bird escape was not pity, as she claimed, but rather a certain joy caused by attacking the property of another. It is for the same reason that she looks at her schoolmates' notebooks. In the malicious pleasure she gets from the mistakes of others, she finds her own superiority; and she believes she is more and better than the others. If she always managed to triumph it would still do nothing for her life. But she will certainly not find anyone who will always offer her this possibility. It is necessary to intervene and attack the trouble at its root. The child must be made to understand the mistake she is making. She must be shown that she has an exaggerated tendency to be superior, and that when she does not succeed in achieving this in a useful way, she tried to assert herself in useless ways (by molesting others and tyrannizing them). But this explanation should not take the form of a reproach, since in this case she would take up her struggle again. A reproach, to a child of this kind, produces a state of mind in which the child thinks: "From now on I'll do it even more." The child wants to prove that she is the strongest after all. I do not believe that this child's error can be eliminated by one conversation. What she needs is for an outsider, who in no way depends upon her, to give her some friendly pointers and show her what is taking place inside her. She knows that her mother defends her, and she does not take seriously her mother's threats to send her away. Being intelligent, she knows the limits beyond which a teacher cannot go; and she knows that there will not be a complete showdown.

We are told that her parents love her, as do her brothers and sisters; despite the fact that she tortures them and treats them meanly. She tries to dominate others; but this does not always succeed with her brothers and sisters—hence her aggressiveness. Everywhere we find the same rhythm and the same structure. The mother's threats are completely futile; and one cannot get results from this child by treating her harshly. She knows that in any case the father is on her side. Moreover, it is likely that he is not entirely responsible for the child's being pampered, since usually the members of a family blame one another for this. It is necessary to give the parents some hints that in reality the child is really not responsible, since up to this time all she could do was follow a style of life established in early childhood. There can be no hope of a change so long as she keeps to her mistaken goal; namely, to be at all times the first and the center of attention.

The best way to enlighten the child, as well as the mother, is to point out that a youngest child very often wants to be the center of attention.

Dr. A.: (to the parents): It doesn't pay to fight with a child, because children are always stronger. You should speak to her in a pleasant way and tell her that if she again starts trying to dominate others (something one very often finds in the youngest child) that there is nothing unusual about this. She must be made to understand where it comes from that she has such a secret urge to be the center of attention at all times.

Advice to the teacher: If and when any relapses occur, look upon them with an understanding smile, and get the child's attention by telling her: "I see you're trying to make yourself the center of attention again."

Dr. A. (to the child, who is crying continuously): Would you like to be the best student? You do lots of things very well. You are an intelligent child. But you must get over the habit of forcing others to pay attention to you all the time. You are the youngest, and you always want to show that you are boss. The youngest child often feels like that, and it's not your fault—we all know that. Now look here. You are good in penmanship, and you are very good in gymnastics. Why should you always be bothering the other girls? You have a good father and a good mother. You could be happy. Is there really any reason why you always have to be the most important one? You can believe me when I tell you there isn't any need for you to cry. You are not here to be punished. You are here so that we can tell you what mistakes you have been making. You always want to show that you are the boss at home. There's no need for that. You know just as much as the others do. You should look people straight in the eye and show them you have a good conscience. Tell yourself: "I don't want to be bossy. I don't want to be unpleasant. I don't want to give my mother extra work so that she'll always have to look after me." Try to please her. You can do it, and then you can tell yourself: "Maybe I'm the youngest, but everybody loves me." What do

you say? Do you think you can do it? Or do you want to go on behaving like somebody who is always saying, "Look at me!"?

Come back in a month.

* 10 *

The Rejected Child

"He was born prematurely (at eight months). Out of wedlock."

The first part of this statement should be regarded with caution.
A child born prematurely, in the eighth month, is not always easy to
distinguish from a child born at the normal time, and it is not always
certain that the diagnosis is accurate. I would advise that the child
not be informed of the fact. Actually, it is of no importance.

"At nine months he was already toddling, and at twelve months he
began to prattle. He cut his first tooth at twelve months."

He should have had his first tooth at six months.

"The other teeth came regularly. Up until now he has had the
measles. The mother could not provide any information on other
diseases he might have had, since the child was with foster parents.
At the time the child's father was a waiter. Now he is living outside
the city, and pays maintenance to the foster parents. The mother
does not have any further information about him. He was coarse,
brutal, and an alcoholic. The mother has a lung condition, according
to the mother, there is no hereditary disease in the family."

We know that hereditary factors should not be taken seriously so
far as mental qualities are concerned.

"The child's mother is married to an unskilled laborer. Their
family life reportedly is good. Two children have been born of this
marriage; one died at the age of one year; the other is three years old.

"The boy was placed with foster parents. The foster father is a
pipefitter at a gas plant. He is an alcoholic, and extremely brutal.
The foster parents have a boy of seventeen and a girl aged two. The
oldest does not get along with the child. He provokes him, gets him
excited, teases him, manhandles him, and beats him at the slightest
provocation. The boy has been given a very bad example, especially
when the father is drunk. At such times there are terrible scenes. He

beats his wife and the children, and it is claimed that one day he threw the little boy about like a ball."

You know what it means to be "a hated child."

"I have had the opportunity to become personally convinced of the deep mark left on a child by these impressions. One day, seeing a boy playing in the sand, I said to the child, 'Be careful not to get your trousers dirty, or your mother will scold you.' To which the child answered: 'My foster father has always scolded my foster mother and me. Sometimes he even beats us with a belt, and then my mother cries.'

"During the father's drunkenness, all the intimacies of family life were enacted before the boy. This fact can be related to the mother's statement that the child had the habit of playing with his penis."

These are manifestations which one frequently finds in children.

"The mother tells of finding him in bed with his three-year-old brother playing with his own penis and with his brother's. The boy was very excited and breathing rapidly. His verbal expressions on this subject are frightful. I have noticed that the boy has a certain tendency to torture animals: he carefully searches for flies and bugs on the window in order to crush them. Once I found him wrapping something around his finger. When I came closer I could see it was an earthworm he had already mutilated and didn't want to give up."

The fact that he tortures animals shows that he has a hostile attitude toward the weak. He looks upon the world as hostile toward him.

"Since April he has been with his own mother, but had to change his environment again when the mother had to go to the hospital for a month. He was placed in a children's home and for two days with a family. On September 25th he entered kindergarten. He is physically neglected and puny, but he does not show any organic abnormalities. His body was covered with eczema, and his head infested with lice. From the kindergarten, the child is taken to the clinic. The mother has been given a course of treatment, but she does not follow it, and his recovery is slow. The mother does not conceal the fact that she does not like the child."

A rejected child: illegitimate.

"During my first interview with the mother, she told me: 'Be severe with the child. I punish him too. You have to speak roughly to him or he won't obey. He's used to it; it's the way he has been treated up to now. Then, too, he is an illegitimate child and has been raised by foster parents. [One has the impression that the mother holds him responsible for the fact that he is an illegitimate child.] He respects me, but he loves my husband more than he does me. When I come close to him he immediately begins to cry. The child keeps me busy all the time. He is unstable and restless, and gets in the way of my work all the time. What gets on his nerves more than anything else is the silence when I am working or at mealtime. To attract attention, he makes little crying sounds, stamps his feet, moves chairs around with a lot of noise, or pounds on the table."

This is hard to believe. It could be imagined only in one case: if he derived sexual excitement when he is being beaten, or when he is scared. Children of this type deliberately provoke the blows they receive. We know that this boy is sexually excitable, and it may be that he belongs to this category.

"When I ask him to be quiet, he laughs at me and goes on making noise. If I don't pay any attention to him, it stimulates him to act even worse. Sometimes he throws himself to the floor and cries without any apparent reason."

One has the impression that he wants to provoke those around him. He knows very well what will happen.

"His rebellion sets a bad example for the group. In fact, when I give a routine order to all of the children, he shouts: 'No! I won't do it!' "

This conduct shows his fighting attitude. He doesn't know that there are people who look upon him with kindness.

"I handle his rebellion differently from that of the other children. But there are some children in the group who take advantage of this and imitate his example."

This kind of behavior is sometimes contagious, especially when the children in question have a strong feeling of inferiority and want to assert themselves. Children want to be equal. You have probably noticed that if one child at school faints, two or three others will also faint.

"He has no social feeling. He stirs up the other children and takes away their toys and building materials, although he has the same toys as the others. He manhandles, scratches, and hits the others for no reason."

He behaves like an enemy.

"He does not have a very clear notion of what belongs to him and what belongs to others."

These notions can be clear only if one has some interest in others.

"An example: The boy takes another child's whistle away from him. The other child comes to me and complains. I try to smooth things over, and advise him to lend his whistle to the boy for a little while. But the child finally insists on his right. I beckon to the boy, but he hides in the most distant corner of the playground. When he finally comes up to me, he throws himself on the ground. I tell him calmly: 'Get up and give the whistle back now. The other child would like to use it a little bit, too. After a while he'll lend it back to you.' The only result of my saying this is that he begins to scream and stamp his feet, and tries to hit me. Seeing what is happening on the playground, a large number of children have crowded around— including those from another group. Since he won't listen, I pick him up from the ground and take him inside. After a while he calms down, and I try to make him understand that he himself wouldn't be pleased if somebody took something away from him. His reaction was astounding. His teeth began to chatter as if he had a chill; and for the rest of that day he stayed close to me, holding my hand which he gently kissed several times. Later, in talking to the mother, I learned that the child's foster parents had taken away every gift given to him and had not returned any of them."

In this scene, it is very remarkable that he behaved so submissively and gratefully. After all, the whistle had been taken away from him; and it is difficult to see why he is grateful. Was he perhaps sexually excited at that moment? Or was he grateful because he had not been beaten?

"Naptime offers one of the greatest difficulties, which makes it very hard for his schoolmates. He disturbs the calm atmosphere by shouting for no reason, getting up suddenly, making noise with his bed, and talking loudly to himself. The other children, who were beginning to go to sleep, or who were asleep already, are awakened."

He behaves like an angry enemy.

"The mother has given us the following information: He has never wet his bed, and he rarely snores. He sleeps with the father, and likes to sleep close to him."

This would seem to confirm the hypothesis that he is sexually excitable.

"He is put to bed at eight o'clock. His sleep is restless, with rapid and sometimes difficult breathing. He wakes up regularly at one o'clock in the morning, and doesn't want to sleep any more. The parents use every means (most frequently, spanking) to make him go back to sleep. When he is home at noon, he is put to bed with his brother, each in his own corner of the bed, and after being spanked a little bit he goes to sleep. This again shows how defeated this child is and how unapproachable. I have tried to influence him by praising his little achievements. He reacts momentarily, but he is not stimulated toward improving his work. During his first few days at kindergarten I noticed when I patted another child he stopped playing, even though he was some distance away."

We must remember that he is in a situation, one he has already experienced many times, where his younger brother is treated more kindly than he is.

"He stood as if transfixed, staring at me. The next day I deliberately began to make the same gesture, quite near him. Again he stood as if paralyzed, and stared at us. I can see what a deep impression this has made on him. My efforts to gain his affection have had little success. It may have some connection with his inability to concentrate. This lack of concentration is manifest in all of his actions."

Here you can see once again that his functions are undeveloped because he does not seek communication with others.

"His words lack order and coherence. If he begins to sweep he will make only a few strokes with the broom, and then put it down and start throwing puppets around. Even during meals this tendency was very noticeable at first. A normal meal, eaten while sitting quietly, is something unknown to him. He requires help when dressing and undressing himself. Recently I have noticed that he is learning to distinguish between right and wrong, because he comes and accuses those children who have done something wrong."

He is seeking contact with the teacher.

"I am not certain that, by telling on the others, he is not trying to see that they are punished.

"He likes to go to kindergarten. The mother says that on Sundays he is always asking to go back to school. Before going to kindergarten he showed no particular excitement. The first few days he even refused to go home."

This clearly shows that he feels better at kindergarten. I have no doubts that in this way he will make progress.

"He cried a great deal, and threw himself on the cloakroom floor. Only our friendly admonition and the promise that he would be able to come back the next day could induce him to get up and go home, together with a little girl from the same neighborhood whose brother is also in kindergarten. His fear of 'home' no longer manifests itself so clearly; but when it is time for him to be picked up and taken home, he seems restless and troubled.

"He impresses one as an alert child. He understands things very well in his own way, and is animated by a strong urge for activity. He is generous. For example, he gave me a plum from his lunch; and a short time later he came back to give me another, saying, 'Here is one more so you will have two.' In general, he likes to give what he has."

Here is something which proves he is beginning to acquire a certain degree of social feeling. It requires some time before a child like this one begins to warm up. It doesn't happen right away. One must be patient; and it is only then that other difficulties can be overcome. I would like to ask the mother whether the boy doesn't provoke his spankings. But it is plain that I must not suggest anything by that. I will try to make her understand in a friendly way that she must engender in the child the feeling that he has as much worth as the others.

* 11 *

An Only Child Seeks to Play a Role

A teacher reports on the case of an eleven-year-old boy who doesn't get along with anyone, and who is constantly interfering with classroom work. He stole some money from his mother. The chief complaint is that he cannot be in the company of other children without quarrelling with them and always playing the leading role. He is an only child.

His school work is average; he seems to be intelligent.

There is no information on the family situation.

An only child, spoiled by too much attention, he cannot relate to other children, a fact which has prevented his social feeling from developing. I would like to talk with the mother.

The mother states that the boy has good qualities but is too much influenced by others. There are times when he does not obey at all. The other boys have reported to the mother that he told them: "I won't do what my mother asks me!" He lies to her frequently, and she punishes him for it. Sometimes her hand "just slips" and at other times she punishes him by taking away something he likes. For a certain length of time he was with foster parents, where he was well treated. At home he is even better treated, and lacks for nothing. Formerly, when he was punished he would apologize. Now he sulks or answers in a sneering way. He would like to play the role of master of the house, and he has a certain tendency to brag. The mother's present husband is not the child's father, but he is very gentle with him. The boy does not know that he is not his father. When the father is at home, the boy behaves even worse, because the father is too good to him. The teachers have advised severity. The boy does not have any friends, because he can't get along with them. He is domineering, and the other children don't like him. He does his lessons all alone.

Last week the mother found that some change was missing from her handbag. She held the boy responsible. He denied having taken the money, but the mother found it on him. She could not find out why he had stolen the money.

He takes pleasure in exchanging and collecting various objects like paper, pictures, pencils, etc. . . . His mother asked him to stop making these "swaps" and promised him instead a little pocket money every week. This pleased him a great deal. Otherwise, the boy is obedient, he willingly helps his mother, and he is quite self-sufficient.

On the subject of his dreams the mother relates that one day, during a boat trip on the Danube, he had a very bad dream which so closely resembled reality that he had wandered to the bridge of the ship before he was finally found. He had dreamed that he was sitting on a chimney and was afraid of falling. When found, he was clinging to a rail. He expressed the desire to become a ship's captain or pilot. And he once remarked: "I would very much enjoy ruling a whole ship."

He is thrifty. His mother complains of his lying and his unsociability. By way of punishment she often spanks him.

Discussion with the mother: The fact that he stole some change is not so very serious, and you shouldn't talk to him about it. It was a very good idea to give him the pocket money. If he knows he can count on this allowance, he will calm down. Personally, I would try not to spank him at all. The boy believes that through his lies and bragging he will be able to attract the attention of others and thus become the center of interest. It would be advisable for you to change and even give up the whole process of punishment. Also, you should make him think of his future and explain to him that to be a captain, in this bragging sense, is no serious profession at all. Let him work by himself, see that he becomes independent. If I were you, I wouldn't go on giving him so much motherly care. He is accustomed to always having you behind him. If he likes gymnastics, let him take part in this sport so that he can mix with other children. I would make him feel that he is no longer a child. This will give him more self-confidence. He has the impression that he is closed in. This was responsible for the most recent incident. He would like to feel that he is somebody, and be convinced that he is playing a meaningful role.

Dr. A. (to the audience, after the mother's departure): This boy likes to play a role, but he is held back by his mother.

Dr. A. (to the boy): You are good at arithmetic. What would you like to be later in life?

The boy: Captain on an ocean liner. I'd like to leave for Hamburg.

Dr. A.: You have to begin as a cabin-boy. How old do you have to be before you can leave for Hamburg?

The boy: Twenty years old.

Dr. A.: You can do it as early as fifteen or sixteen. But in the meantime, and before you become captain, you have to learn many things. Why do you like that profession so much? Have you already been on a ship? What is it that you like so much about it?

The boy: That you can order others around.

Dr. A.: Where do you order around now? Do you do it with your mother or in school?

The boy: I do order the children around.

Dr. A.: If you want to be captain, you have to give intelligent orders so that everybody will say you are doing the right thing. But at school, with the other children, you aren't the captain, and it doesn't fit that you give orders there. I don't understand why you want to give orders at school. Because of that, you probably don't have any friends. The other children are right: they aren't there for you to give orders to them. You can give orders later. Right now, try to be nice and make friends. The captain of a ship is also friendly with the passengers. He has to know other things besides how to give orders. He has to have friends too. If the others don't like him, or perhaps hate him, they won't obey. You must learn to be nice to the other children. Giving orders is a kind of bragging. You like to trade things and buy things. You like to do something important. You always want to have the others think you are captain. Do you remember anything else that made a deep impression on you when you were very young?

The boy: Once I saw them putting a bell up to the top of a tower. I was about three or four years old.

Dr. A.: Did you like that?

The boy: I liked seeing how the men were hanging there.

Dr. A.: You liked seeing how you can get higher up? I would like you to have some friends. Wouldn't you like to go to the child care center? Perhaps your mother will let you learn gymnastics, too. People can learn anything. You could do your lessons at the child care center—that would be rather enjoyable. What are you going to do with the money you are saving?

The boy: If some day I am in need, I'll have something.

Dr. A.: Are you afraid that you might be in need? That you might fall down? If you are a hard worker, that's the best way to avoid poverty. You know, having money isn't the most important kind of security. Do you like to brag, too?

The boy: Yes.

Dr. A.: You should get rid of that habit. If a person wants to be captain he shouldn't lie. Your mother and teacher both love you. If you learn well and become a decent man, you can become anything you want. If you want to be a captain you have to build a good foundation.

Come back in a month and tell me if you have made some friends, if you have stopped interfering with teacher's work in the classroom, and if you still want to give orders.

* 12 *

The Oldest Child Dethroned

"I have two boys, aged seven and nine respectively. I cannot yet judge the work of the younger boy, since he is in the first grade."

Here we have two boys, an older and a younger. We know that each child in a family grows up under different conditions. We must not assume that they grow up in identical situations. In this case the older boy was the only child for two years. As such, he was probably the center of attention and pampered. The entire household was at his beck and call. Suddenly a second child appears, and the situation changes completely. The older boy has been trained by experience that he can have everything his way, like a king. Then suddenly the mother's attention is transferred to the second child. She does not have as much time for the older boy as before. Since it is not easy to prepare an older child for the arrival of another, we shall find that in fact this boy was not prepared. He is faced with a difficult test. At such times, many children are consumed with jealousy and begin a bitter struggle to gain their parents' attention and recover the previous more favorable situation. The second child is in a totally different situation: he is never alone. He has someone he can follow, whom he wants to follow, and even catch up with. A child once said to me: "If I'm so sad, it's because I'll never be as old as my big brother." (Cf. Esau and Jacob.)

The older boy experienced a real tragedy when the younger was born. If we should hear now that he is constantly afraid that the second child will catch up with him or even surpass him, and that he has lost all hope, we will understand that this attitude is due to his already automatic way of thinking about it. Engraved on his soul is the notion: "Suddenly someone comes and takes everything away from me."

The attitude will vary from one child to another. It depends upon the following factors: First, the extent to which the child's style of life has developed up to that point, and the difficulty or ease with which it can be modified. Second, the behavior of the younger child. Third, the behavior of the parents. Last, the extent to which the parents have prepared the older child, and how far they have extended his social feeling toward others. These are important factors which we must consider.

Now we shall see how this older boy is developing. "In my opinion the older boy is slow in learning."

This is the hesitant attitude. We can deduce from this that the boy believes he cannot make any progress; he has lost his courage. He knows that he can't get ahead on the useful side of life. His striving for recognition will be manifested on the useless side. Laziness signifies: "He gives me trouble, thus I must pay attention to him." In a twisted way, he has achieved what he always wanted: to attract more attention, to have others spend more of their time on him. Laziness in learning means distance from the solution of given tasks. It is an attitude of hesitation. When you consider the automatic style of life of lazy children, you find that their behavior differs from that of a child who is self-confident. They will often tell you, "I don't think of myself as more stupid than the others' but I'm just not interested." If this particular boy were expecting success, he would not be lazy. Laziness indicates a low opinion of oneself. It also contains the striving to gain recognition. Lazy children are usually the center of attention. They have given themselves an ambitious task: to induce those around them to pay more attention to them. We should not be surprised, in questioning a boy of this type about his laziness, if he replied: "Don't you see? I am the laziest boy in my class, but people always pay attention to me and they are always kind and nice to me. The boy next to me works hard, and nobody pays any attention to him." He profits by his laziness.

The least bit of good work he does is immediately praised. If he does not do well, he is told: "If you weren't lazy, you could be the best." It is astounding to see the extent to which a lazy child can be satisfied with the feeling that he could be the best. He doesn't even want to try. Here we find, once again, the striving for recognition on the useless side of life.

"No exhortations, whether kindly or severe, have so far yielded any results."

The boy does not know what is happening inside of him. He is acting in accordance with his own style of life. He is like a man in a trap. The fact that he lets himself be exhorted, shows only that actually he wants to be the center of attention. Certain children will take thrashings willingly, because they can then experience the triumph of having irritated their fathers. Some children even experience pleasure in being spanked—a pleasure which may sometimes have a sexual content.

"He promises only that he will work harder."

There you see: "I want to."

"But he doesn't do anything about it. During their writing, he allows himself to be distracted by anyone or anything."

He feels that he cannot make others appreciate him through working. He is following a different course.

"He is interested in everything but his lessons. In order to make his work easier, I instructed him to report to me on what he had learned during the day at school."

Once again we see him in the foreground. Every evening he talks with his father—with God.

"But when I come home in the evening, he does not show up to keep his promise."

The father has to remember it himself.

"He doesn't tell me unless I ask him directly. Then he says: 'I don't know.' "

We know he believes that in this area he will not gain any recognition. We must encourage him and show him that if he takes the trouble he can be outstanding, even in his studies.

"The subjects which are the hardest for him are grammar, arithmetic, and penmanship, and these are the ones he most detests."

Perhaps an additional element in his marked feeling of inferiority is the fact that he is left-handed.

This would be important to ascertain. I would like to call your attention to the fact that among those who have trouble with arithmetic you will find mostly pampered children, those who need a crutch. In all other subjects there are some helpful aids. But in arithmetic everyone must work independently and think independently. Pampered children are usually ill prepared for arithmetic.

"His great reluctance to get down to work proves his antipathy toward these subjects. He seems to have more interest in natural history. It would also appear that he likes to draw; but he produces only horrible caricatures. Apparently he lacks talent."

Probably he is a left-handed child!

"He can remain sitting or lying down for hours at a time, just looking off into space."

Time is the greatest enemy of such children who have a poor opinion of themselves. This boy has found a way to pass the time: he "looks off into space."

"Although he has a great many books and has started to read several of them, he has never finished one."

No patience, no perseverance! No one is solicitous of him; he cannot expect anything from others.

"He looks around for toys; then after a short time he abandons them without having had any enjoyment.

"The social situation of this child—or rather, of both children—is not very good, although they are not suffering from hunger.

"The saddest thing in their lives is probably the fact that they spend the day in a children's home."

This is a risky assumption. We would like to find the true situation and give the boy some encouragement.

"The head-mistress of this home has a particular animosity against my oldest child, since she is an ardent religionist and we do not belong to any church. She told me that he lied, and was sly and lazy, and that this was because he had been reared outside the church."

We have no doubt that these attitudes are brought about by his lack of hope. I must confess that this boy, who does not belong to a church, can be improved even in a clerical children's home only if he is encouraged. If the headmistress says that the boy's attitude stems from the fact that he was reared outside the church, she hardly seems to have the proper understanding for finding this child's weak spot.

The father adds: "To tell the truth, I myself have found that he has all these bad character traits, whereas the younger boy has no faults, and people say only good things about him. The only criticisms they have to make are about the older boy."

All these things show that the older boy has been pushed into the background by his younger brother.

Is it a matter of chance that the older boy developed in the wrong direction and the younger brother in the right direction? Certainly not. The older brother believes the younger one has pushed him out of the situation which was so pleasant formerly. And the more friendship and love he loses, the more discouraged he becomes. The younger boy, who is at present the victor, is aware that he is in a pleasant situation, and he has no need to attract unfavorable attention.

* 13 *

Lying: a Way of Gaining Recognition

I have here an opportunity of presenting to you the case history of a problem child whose mother was already somewhat familiar with our ideas. You will be able to see how she faces the problem, how far her understanding goes, and how she tries to cooperate with us— although she knows that it won't be very easy for her.

"My son Philip, nine years of age, is what they call a problem child."

This probably means that he makes problems for her, that he gives her a lot of trouble, and that he displays a behavior which is not compatible with social feeling. We would have no reason to rack our brains and try to educate children if the always present social feeling would not rebel against failures of this kind.

If the mother tells us, "He is nervous," this does not mean very much. In general, when people use this term they mean that the child is restless and difficult to deal with. I would like to call your attention to the fact that a special sensitivity is the most important element of neurosis. This sensitivity may not always manifest itself as such, but it can be manifested in its consequences. It is the latter case that we are dealing with here, and we shall see that in this child the consequence of the sensitivity will be manifested in an attempt to achieve increased importance. This is what is called in America (under the influence of Individual Psychology) "the superiority complex." Now of course this is already the second phase, the result of the "inferiority complex"; viz., of the feeling of inferiority. You can understand that hyper-sensitivity comes into play between these two. A child who is very sensitive will regard his situation as a defeat. Consequently, he will try to find a way out of it. He will look for compensation, and produce feelings of superiority.

"He is terribly restless."

This confirms the fact that, in his situation, he cannot find rest.

"He doesn't learn anything."

This is somewhat jumbled and must be understood and interpreted in a different sense. The boy does not feel equal to the requirements of school, and hence makes no effort there.

"However, he is not stupid; and he sometimes surprises people by his good judgment."

We can understand this very well. We have assumed merely that this child felt incompetent when faced with the requirements of school. He has the ability to take on other problems. As far as we can see, we cannot count him among the courageous children. We know that such children have little interest in others, but a great deal in themselves.

"He misses nothing of what goes on in the street."

I am afraid that a great many modern psychologists would casually ignore such a remark. We are justified in assuming that this is a boy who takes an interest in everything visual. And this explains a great many things. If his interest is only visual, this is an advantage when is comes to lessons which embody demonstrations, but he will have less of a tendency to listen. This is important at school; and many setbacks may be due to this mechanism. We will bear in mind the fact that he is one of those children who satisfy their visual tendencies first of all. If you think about the question: When can one do if one is content just to look at things? you will find that one cannot do very much that is useful, and in any case not very much in which the social feeling can be manifested. You will think of drawing, of painting, perhaps of a better understanding of the visible world. The problem is not very easy, when someone has accentuated one aspect of life to this extent. Actually, under these conditions there does not remain sufficient interest in the other necessities of existence, and the individual can no longer develop in this direction. This boy has not been properly prepared for school, and it is not his fault. But he takes a great deal of interest in everything that is visual—in all external appearances. If we are on the right track, even in an incomplete description of his life we can hope to find confirmations of our assumptions.

"He remembers everything adults say."

Let us emphasize this fact; it shows us his interest in everything adult. Here we see very clearly his striving for recognition—his desire also to be big.

"And he can repeat it accurately, at just the right time."

We are beginning to get a certain amount of information about the style of life of this nine-year-old boy. But we still lack confirmations and indications as to the specific variant of this type.

"But he is cowardly."

This is not new to us.

"He is afraid of everything, and he runs away from any kind of danger."

He has no self-confidence whatsoever. We may assume that the mother plays an important role. He is not independent; he does not try to solve his own problems. Moreover, he has no intention of facing them, since so far he has been used to having his mother stand behind him. At this point, we are better able than any of the other schools of psychology to establish the fact that he is a pampered child. These children play a very important role and account for a large proportion of problem children, nervous individuals, potential suicides, drunkards, criminals, and sexual perverts. This fact is so important that I want to add a few words and define what we mean by "pampered child." (Mothers often say, "Sometimes I spank the child." They imagine that by saying this they can avoid the suspicion of having pampered the child.) Let me say immediately that by this term we do *not* imply any sexual attachment. A pampered child is one who has been relieved of his independent functioning. Someone else speaks for him, recognized the dangerous situations, and protects him from them. In short, the child is taken in tow by someone else. He has another person at his disposal, and he builds his life in symbiosis with her. Such a child has a parasitic trait: he tries to get everything he wants through the aid of his mother.

"He knows very well that cowardice is something ugly, and now he makes up the worst kind of lies."

We can guess what kind of lies these are, since he is urged on to make a grand appearance, to be recognized and esteemed. Since we know he listens to what adults say, there is little doubt that in his lies he will play the role of a hero.

"For example, he says: 'I was in England. From where I was standing I looked around the corner of a wall, and I saw a tiger.' "

In itself, this is a big lie. But what interests me particularly is that he does not just look, he looks "around the corner of a wall." This is virtuosity. Not everyone can do it. And it tells us even more: the boy's interest is particularly marked, and he is eager to conquer difficulties—difficulties which would be insurmountable for anyone else. In this connection we should remember that in such cases we are usually dealing with children who have suffered from an inferior visual apparatus. If now I tell you that this boy is cross-eyed, you will understand the source of his interest for everything visual—why he has become what, in modern phraseology, is termed 'eidetic.' This cross-eyed boy's urge to accomplish acrobatic feats in the visual sphere is betrayed in his expression of wanting to look "around the corner of the wall."

"Once when I came home the door was open. Nobody dared to go in, since there was a thief in the closet. I took the hatchet and killed him."

Here, again, he "sees" something, and he accomplishes a deed of heroism. The mother states accurately:

"He always wants to play the role of hero. He wants to be the person everybody admires and who can do everything. If he says, 'Today at school nobody knew anything but me,' I am certain that things went badly at school. And this is all confirmed regularly."

At this point I would like to clarify his mode of compensating, although it is sufficiently apparent. He seems to compensate in his imagination, and then everything gets lost in the void. He does not become active in his compensation. This is another example of what we expressed previously: he is cowardly. He is used to being helped by his mother, who does everything for him.

"I understand him. I know he would like to be a good student and a brave boy. I have already learned that he lies only to increase his sense of personality."

In this comment you will already recognize the viewpoint of Individual Psychology.

"I don't punish him."

We agree with the mother completely. This boy, who despairs in every way of his knowledge and his strength—who, when he must accomplish something, always feels as though he were on the edge of an abyss, and draws back with good reason—does not deserve to be punished. We can see already what should be done. He should be helped along far enough so that he takes courage again, and learns that problems can be solved. He will develop if he dares to strive forward. But as long as his goal is to gain recognition on the useless side of life, as long as he avoids solving his problems on the useful side of life, nothing will be accomplished. He will use everything to prove that there is nothing for him to do on the useful side. We understand why a child like this should not be punished. For him, punishment would only be a confirmation of his inability; and he would find other ways to escape punishment and to draw back from the abyss at the same time.

"I love the little boy."

This is a confirmation we had been lacking. It proves that the mother pampers the child.

"I love him with all my heart. But he lies. He lies more and more, and he is afraid his lies will be discovered."

Here we see the emergence of a hope—of the possibility that some day, out of fear, he will stop lying and approach the truth. But what happens in this case to his goal of superiority? Is this the only conclusion such a boy can draw? No, there is another: to construct his lies with such skill and refinement that he can hope they will never be discovered. This is the path he must take. There is no other, since he cannot completely lose his sense of personality. He became a liar in order to represent something. Therefore, we understand that he cannot give up his lying and run the risk of appearing to be a "zero" —a negligible quantity. What he will do in fact is to have recourse to more subtle lies.

"My husband says I spoil him."

This is something you will always meet up with. If by the sweat of your brow you have discovered the style of life of your subject, you will always find someone in his entourage who has already said it. Does this not remind you of the behavior of our adversaries in psychology who insist that they said the same thing themselves, and who believe that, once having said it, they have achieved a result? It is quite true; the child is pampered. But does he understand the connection? Even if he knew that every child has a striving for recognition, would he be able to analyze how it was created in him? Merely to say that the child is pampered does not mean that anything has yet been accomplished. People don't know what to do with this word. Mothers are right when they say, "How can I avoid spoiling him?" This question makes sense as long as the mother herself has not yet grasped the context as we see it in this case.

". . . My husband claims that this is why the boy is so unstable and such a liar, and furthermore he thinks the boy is 'touched in the head' since my father married a cousin."

A blood relationship between the grandparents has been discovered. Was I not right in maintaining that no one had accomplished anything merely by calling him a pampered child, as the father did? The father himself does not believe in this, and is looking for a second reason which is more convincing. He attributes the child's instability to the fact of a blood relationship among his antecedents.

You can see to what extent science has facilitated things for the father, who can thus make the mother responsible for the child's failures and brilliantly escape any blame on himself.

"That marriage between blood relatives is the curse of my life. He constantly throws it up to me. In other families, too, it happens that one child is more difficult than another. But my husband continues to insist that the marriage between blood relatives was responsible. I must prove to him that this isn't true. I must make something of the boy. He is not bad. On the contrary, he is good-hearted."

It is likely that his good-heartedness is only an aspect of his cowardice. You can see that we are profoundly correct in maintaining that one cannot isolate one particular element of a style of life, that everything has many sides. Kindness may very well represent something negative: "beauty becomes ugliness, ugliness becomes beauty." It is because of this diversity that no one can come to understand a human being's inner workings unless he has first grasped his style of life.

"He even gives his belongings to other children for no other reason than to gain their favor."

You can see that this kindness involves a streak of egoism. He tries to bribe other children in order to be pampered by them.

"He gives away things that are dear to him; and he loves his father, although his father is not nice to him."

At this point I would like to add that in one respect the boy is already showing a certain variant: he is already at a stage where he wants to win over not only his mother but others as well. As we have already established, he tries to obtain protection for himself, and he would like to be appreciated and admired. This is also the goal of his lying.

"For example, it is a big occasion for him when he goes out with his father. I am asking your advice. Should I be severe? I don't believe this brings results. He cries, and promises everything; and then ten minutes later he has forgotten all about it."

The mother has tried to be strict, but obviously without result, since the only possible method was to make him understand the mistakes he makes in building his style of life. Practically, this means: to make him independent and autonomous; to awaken his self-confidence. So long as this is not done, either severity or kindness seems useless, although we prefer kindness. This boy is not prepared. It is cruel to demand something from someone for which he has not been prepared. With animals, we are always ready to measure exactly what they can do, and not to demand more and not to force it. But with human beings we are not concerned with these matters. Think for a moment of the importance of this remark as applied to school, where children arrive with varying degrees of preparation. To employ the system of grading which, basically, evaluates the child's preparation and not his aptitudes, is therefore "putting them all in the same boat."

"And so he is obliged to lie, since he becomes more and more entangled in his lies."

Without expressing herself clearly, the mother means that he cannot find any other way to make himself appreciated.

She asked for advice, and I advised her in accordance with what I have briefly indicated to you in the foregoing.

But perhaps there are more items of importance in the rest of the report.

"Recently, when he started to lie again, I pretended it was a joke and laughingly explained why he was lying."

In this "why" you will recognize the indications I gave to the mother.

"Philip, admitting his lie, became embarrassed and started to laugh."

The boy is profoundly aware that his lie is a lie. He is conscious of it. We are going to set up a test for those authors who claim they have established a difference between the conscious and the unconscious, and believe that bad instincts are found in the unconscious and penetrate into the conscious only through a censor and in a veiled form, as it were. What does this lie mean? If we understand the conscious and do accept the lie not simply as a lie, we know that it is a means of attracting attention. If we examine this boy with respect to his unconscious, we shall see that he is harboring there a strong feeling of inferiority which is seeking to liberate itself. Based on this feeling of inferiority is his striving for recognition. So that it is in no way different from what we also see in the conscious.

"Of course, I make mistakes. Recently Philip asked his father to take him to the cemetery. He had to write a theme for school. My husband refused, and the maid went with him. The next day his theme turned out to be very good, but there was not a word of truth in it."

I would like to remark in passing that a theme doesn't necessarily have to be true. But the mother is right if she finds in the theme the same behavior pattern she sees in his lies.

"He recounted in detail how he went to the cemetery with his father, and how his father cried. At the end he said: 'I didn't cry. A man doesn't cry.' "

He surpassed his father—though only in his imagination. His mother understands that very well.

"So he humbled his father and made himself important, lying all the time."

"He humbled his father and made himself important." Is there anyone among our contemporaries who does not remember the so-called Oedipus complex? The question now is: Does the boy have an Oedipus complex in his subconscious? Was that why he humbled his father and had him cry at the cemetery? Or are his strivings directed toward making himself important and to outdo the father, who resists him? Might it not be that premature sexual ideas are developing out of the Oedipus complex, which is also located in the conscious? This is a question for reflection. But as Individual Psychologists we do not hesitate. We see that the line of striving runs, from below to above, through an entire life and this includes the development of sexuality.

"But the theme was good, and the teacher complimented Philip, and after the class, he read the theme to me. I didn't have the heart to expose the boy. I said nothing, and pretended to have paid no attention."

This concludes the report on the boy in question. We can say with good reason that he belongs to a very common type: the liar who wants to make himself important. This striving is a very frequent tendency in children, because of their smallness. Think for a moment about the basic situation of this boy: pampered by his mother and put in second place by his father. What he was able to acquire from his mother had no value outside the family circle. We can assume that children who are afflicted with strabismus are not especially liked. They learn this quickly, and as a result they will regard the world as hostile. It is not surprising that this boy, very early in life, became aware of this resistance and of the fact that things are different on the outside than they are with his mother. His response was flight. Since no one can escape from his own striving for superiority, he had to find the line along which he would operate: bragging and lying. There are other forms as well; but in all of them you will find the striving to get out of an inferior position (for example, by distorting the facts when threatened with punishment), to recover self-importance by a trick, and rise again. In other lies, in bragging, we can always establish the fact that they involve things which make the child feel incompetent, and which he tries to escape through his fantasy. It is as though he were trying to stand on tip-toe. You can understand how wrong it is to hand out severe punishment for this attempt, which results from a real need. The only thing which will prove fruitful is explanation. "You don't have to run away, you don't have to resort to lies, you don't have to brag. If you really want to make an effort—you can satisfy your strivings for recognition by doing useful things, and you won't have to resort to foolish tricks."

* **14** *

"The Hero Role in Phantasy"

A Substitute for Useful Accomplishment in Reality

The teacher reports that the case we are going to discuss is that of a boy who was in his second grade class. This boy is nine years old and is manifesting aggressive behavior.

This information does not make it clear whether the child was nine years old when he first entered the second grade. A boy of nine should already be in the third grade.

"When he entered school he was still scrawling. It was only little by little that he learned to write."

We remember that his behavior is rude. Probably he has the temperament of a fighter. It is likely that he belongs to that category of people who swear by the ideal of the hero, the "code of honor." Why was it so hard for him to learn to write? We are inclined to think he is left-handed, but this is not certain.

"His weakest point is arithmetic."

Here, again, we are not on solid ground. Perhaps he is one of those pampered children who have difficulty in arithmetic, since this subject offers no crutch. In other subjects there are rules, and one can learn something by heart. In arithmetic it is useless, except for the multiplication table. Since pampered children never want to do anything on their own, we are not surprised to find so many poor arithmetic students among them. If we can prove this statistically, the belief in a "gift for arithmetic" will have been undermined.

"He is taking remedial work in this subject."

This is a substitute for being pampered.

"He likes these supplementary classes very much."

We do not know why. Perhaps the teacher is very kind. Perhaps the child finds realized in these classes the conditions he demands of classroom work; namely, that he be pampered.

"He likes to have special attention paid to himself."

This is the first confirmation that he is a child who wants to be pampered. Other confirmations follow:

"He asks for help when getting dressed. He is brought to school and taken home after school. He never comes to school or goes home alone. And yet he is big and well developed for his age. He has red hair."

It is known that red hair exposes children to teasing which is painful to them. This applies more to boys than to girls, since red hair belonging to a girl is often considered pretty. By contrast, red-haired boys are not especially liked. These are archaic, superstitious reactions which create a great deal of damage since we often do find red-headed children among those with minor failures. It is a fact I have seen confirmed from different sources. But these are not failures of a serious nature. One has the impression that in the long run these red-haired boys overcome their difficulties despite everything. While it is not especially pleasant to be the object of teasing outside the home, things are different within the family. The feeling of inferiority is not very pronounced.

"If he does a job poorly and his mother criticizes him, he becomes furious."

This means that he has been able to establish between himself and his mother a relationship which makes her dependent. He achieves this by means of his rage—or perhaps also by being spanked. This happens frequently, because with pampered children there comes a point where the pampering has to stop. Therefore they are threatened automatically with an aggravation of their situation when they grow up.

"If he is praised, he encourages himself by telling himself that things will turn out all right."

Here we have proof that he is not completely discouraged.

"He has learned to speak and to walk normally."

We can conclude from this that he has not encountered any difficulties in his organic development.

"Since the age of eighteen months he has shown signs of rage."

If this observation is accurate, we must remember it. Personally I have been able to ascertain these signs even in a child of six months. He was a bottle-fed baby who developed very well, took his feedings regularly, and did not present any problems in this area. When he was six months old, the following peculiarity was observed. Upon awakening from his sleep the baby would whimper softly. If you came up to him with the bottle and he could get his liquid, he behaved perfectly. But if you came to him without the bottle he would begin to scream furiously, with manifest signs of rage. The family had got into the habit of always bringing the bottle when going to the baby.

"At first he seemed very depressed at school."

We can understand this very readily: he was looking for a situation in which he could make others pamper him. He wanted to be the center of attention—to control things. At school, he has no such opportunities. Thus, such children will act depressed. It is a sign of a pampered child. With the aid of Individual Psychology, teachers can very easily get a picture of a child. They can build on this foundation—not, of course, without looking for confirmations and making the corrections that prove necessary.

"He has a fertile imagination."

We can conclude from this that he is not on good terms with the inhibiting reality. He builds for himself an imaginary world in which he lives at ease. There he finds tranquility, he is powerful, he can satisfy his desire to give orders. In such a world he can imagine conquests, victorious battles, and the acquisition of an immense fortune with which he can reward and save others. Such children also consider themselves at times as saviours of important personalities. In their imaginations they catch run-away horses, they save the king or his daughter, and jump into the water to save princesses—who of course prove to be very grateful. When they find themselves back on the *terra firma* of reality, these children are very depressed.

"His thoughts are full of stories about Indians and bandits."

He is a hero in his own phantasy. You may be sure that this boy is a coward. This is an attempt on his part to compensate.

"He is always ready to fight against an invisible enemy."

These phantasies could be put to good use; the boy can train himself psychologically against his cowardice. Some children certainly succeeded by this means in ridding themselves at least partially of their cowardice.

"Sometimes his imagination runs away with him. He will tell his mother of imaginary events at school, and at the end he will say: 'You know, Mamma, that didn't really happen. I made it up.' "

Here, again, we find a small amount of social feeling. He doesn't want to be taken for a liar. He keeps control of the reality within his range. If he didn't, this would be neurotic lying. Even if children become very excited about the game they are playing, they know what they owe to reality. The things this boy imagines and then tells about, prove that he wants to stand on tip-toe and appear bigger than he is. We can conclude from this that he has a depressing feeling of inferiority, which agrees with the designation of pampered child that we gave him.

"His mother reports that he was very sick in his early childhood: intestinal colic at four months, scrofula later on, and a weak lung."

We are not in a position to evaluate this, nor to say how right the mother is in considering this child as very sick. What interests us more is the fact that, having considered him very sick, she must have given him special care and love in raising him. She must have made this child extremely dependent upon her.

"She says that if a child is sick he must be handled with care."

She expresses in another way what we have just said.

"He is afraid of the dark."

Here we have the signs of the pampered child. To be afraid of the dark means: Someone has to stay near me.

"He is very clumsy."

This again raises our suspicion that he may be left-handed.

"His sister who is eight years older than he, has a bad influence on his clumsiness."

We learn that he has a sister eight years older than he is, and we can assume that she does not behave toward him as a sister, but as a mother or aunt. Since he cannot very well consider her as a rival, the boy is growing up like an only child.

"She interferes with his efforts, criticizing and berating him."

She is like a critical mother—one might say like a step-mother.

"He is very aggressive . . ."

He knows that his mother is behind him to defend him. And he knows that if he gets into a fight with his sister, she will not be able to get very far.

". . . especially against those who are stronger than he is."

This information is a bit startling. I am not inclined to believe that it is entirely accurate. If it is only partly accurate, the child is not completely discouraged: he believes he is capable of something. But this is still not heroism, since the stronger ones are probably (like his sister) members of the family. It may also be that he attacks the teacher, who seems strong to us but does not necessarily seem so to the boy. He may have the feeling that the teacher exists for him.

"He is often teased because of the color of his hair. At such times he goes into a rage."

As we have seen, he is a pampered child, who, as much through his sister's fault as owing to the color of his hair, is regularly in a state of irritation. One can also send an animal into a rage by constantly irritating it, and the same thing is true of this boy.

"He talks in his sleep, and he sleeps fitfully."

We have always found these signs in pampered children.

"He is very restless when he is doing his lessons."

If we were to interpret this we would say that his lessons place him in a tense situation, and that this tension shows in his restlessness.

"He is quarrelsome."

We can understand this: he is in a chronic state of irritation.

"But he is also compassionate."

This is not a contradiction. I do not see why, although unyielding toward his enemy, he should not be kind to someone who is suffering. A person who sees a contradiction here, believes in the theory of ambivalence. For our part, we say that the same style of life expresses itself differently in different situations.

"He showed his pity one day when his sister was hurt in the head."

On that occasion she was a conquered enemy. Here we also see that he has retained a certain amount of social feeling, and that he is capable of behaving with humanity in a proper situation.

"He is very concerned about getting to school on time."

I would not dare to interpret this without further investigation. If I would have to connect this with what we already know, I would say: He is trying to get ahead; he wants to demonstrate the importance of school. This conforms to his eagerness in taking remedial classes. He is not too discouraged. He would like to be a victor some day.

"The mother herself is very nervous and loses her patience easily."

Here is a new difficulty for a boy who is in a chronic state of irritation. Now we can better understand why he often becomes furious.

"During the day the father is at the theatre, where he works as an electrician. The mother runs the family."

Here, too, he turns against the strongest one.

"The mother is a big, shrewish woman with an air of great self-importance, as is the sister. Throughout the child's upbringing they have criticized him constantly."

This is further grounds for attack, provoked by the mother, who makes the boy even more irritable.

"The father is good to him."

It would seem to me quite normal that the boy should ally himself more with the father, which would represent the second phase. During the first part of his life he was certainly closer to the mother, since he was a sick child. She must have cared for him and pampered him. It is likely that later on he was unable to maintain this bond between them.

"If he wants something and doesn't get it, he cries until his desire is satisfied."

He is obstinate, and he knows that his tears make an impression. We find this trait in many children and in many adults. They have the impression that their tears are an invincible weapon. Also, there are people who cannot bear to see someone cry. They must either satisfy the desire of the one who cries, or else they themselves show signs of extreme agitation. Either one suffices for the person who is crying.

"The mother says: 'I am more severe with him, but my husband gives in on everything.'"

We know that this is not the right way to do things, since the child, who is already attached to his father, will tend to exclude his mother' even more. It would be better if the parents could agree on a policy which would satisfy both of them. They must help each other.

"I don't always give in."

This confirms what we already know.

"The brother and sister often quarrel. The sister has her faults, too. She always irritates him. But he always wants to be right, and he is very bossy."

Moreover he is the youngest child, and as such he employs great efforts and perseverance to surpass the others. If difficulties appear, he tries to get around them in some easier way. The youngest child always manages to find a way which assures his domination over the others, for better or for worse.

"The boy would like to be an electrician like his father."

The father represents a stage in his ideal strivings for superiority. The fact that he wants to become what his father is, shows his admiration for him. He believes that his father's profession represents quite simply a god-likeness.

"But he would also like to be a hunter."

We can understand this desire stems from his tendency to play the hero. But he will never play this role to the end. He would like to hunt defenseless animals, which is not precisely the role of the hero.

"His favorite toys are firearms. He doesn't have a friend."

Here we see the character trait of a pampered child who has not succeeded in forming friendships with other children. He spoils everything with his tendency to dominate.

"He doesn't get along with anybody. He is a kill-joy."

He doesn't have any self-confidence, even when it is a matter of being the leader in a game. He prefers to be a kill-joy.

"His phantasy always connects with something in reality."

A vague piece of information, since one may say the same thing of all phantasy. It is impossible to invent something that is not based on reality.

"Recently he always wants to go into the jungle."

He is probably the master of the jungle, armed with cannons. (The animals don't have any weapons.)

"He practices his hero roles in front of the mirror."

This suggests that he might some day take up an acting career. This may even be the habitual pattern. At the outset of his career, every actor probably wanted to play the role of hero. It seems unlikely that a girl would dream of playing a funny old lady rather than, say, Joan of Arc.

"He brandishes his wooden sword in front of the mirror. And when he is through, he says with satisfaction: 'Now everything has been smashed.' "

Here we see the same trait we have found in many children. They train themselves in a particular aptitude, and identify with a situation. They behave as if they were really playing the role of hero. They are filled with the feeling that they are what they want to be. Every human being is capable of doing that. It is manifested when reality becomes too limiting, when a person meets difficulties in his strivings toward superiority. In this boy's case the resistance is plain to see: he is bothered by his sister, and criticized by his mother. Outside the home he is teased because of his red hair; and at school he does not play a brilliant role. Suppose someone posed this problem for us: Let us assume that you are nine years old, that no one thought well of you either at home or outside, and that in addition you were the youngest child. What would you do? There would be only one possibility: to take refuge in phantasy; to find there what reality refuses to give us. I ask you to remember: to behave in this way is not logical. The intelligence of an adult, especially of a teacher, would furnish objections: this boy should make more of an effort at school. We do not know for certain that he did not make an effort. Perhaps he did, without getting results. We can understand that this does not seem easy to the boy. It may be that he is left-handed without knowing it, which would mean that he is combatting very real difficulties. Knowing that he approached life with a pampered style, and that he assimilates everything in accordance with such a style, we should say: He is behaving in a perfectly intelligent fashion. There is no mistake in what he is doing. We say this because we can identify with him. If I were in this boy's place I would experience exactly the same difficulties, and I would probably behave in the same way. This proves that the boy is neither feeble-minded nor guilty. He is in a difficult situation, with no way out.

Treatment, then, can succeed under different conditions; for example, if the boy became a better student. This result is possible through remedial help. He would certainly improve if his mother and sister were not allowed to give orders to him—at least for a certain length of time—and if one could make them understand that they have harmed the boy. They should try to help him. This should be explained to them in a friendly way. Otherwise one runs the risk that these two aggressive women might turn against the counselor. The most important thing is to make the boy independent, and to encourage him. It is not necessary to be an expert in education or psychology in order to encourage someone. But it will not be an easy task. The boy has become bogged down in the conviction that he will never be able to play an important role except in his phantasy. It would be very useful if we could find a friend for him who was capable of recognizing his good qualities.

The only sure way is treatment by Individual Psychology. We must draw the boy's attention to what has happened. We must show him that a person who always tries to be the center of attention will always be exposed to being hurt. He must seek satisfaction on the useful side of life. For example, he should take part in games instead of being a kill-joy. We should show him that among mankind there are many injustices, and that people often find ways of oppressing others. This goes on everywhere in the same way. One nation wants to humble another, one family believes it is superior to another, certain things are emphasized in order to find a point of attack. But this can happen only as long as the other party lends itself to it. The boy must understand that he should not offer a target to others by letting himself be irritated by them. It is the same elsewhere in life: if someone shows he is annoyed, the attacker persists. The boy should consider the attacks he undergoes because of his red hair as a sign of stupidity on the part of the one who launches them.

I have had the opportunity of talking with a great many people belonging to oppressed races—with Negroes and Jews. I have called their attention to the general tendency to depreciate one's neighbor. Everyone tries to find something which will give him a cheap sense of superiority. One cannot deny that the Frenchman considers the German as an inferior, while the German thinks he belongs to a chosen nation. The Chinese has contempt for the Japanese. Persons who travel a great deal have found that human beings are more or less the same everywhere in that they always incline to find some way of belittling others. This can still be seen between the bourgeois and the proletarian. Is there one single human being who has not been aware of the jealousy and envy that others feel toward him? Why should we take it seriously if someone belittles us because of our national origin, religion, or the color of our hair? This is only the crystallization of a common tendency—of a generalized obsessional neurosis.

Until humanity decides to take a step forward in its degree of civilization we must necessarily consider these hostile tendencies not as specific symptoms but as the expression of a general and mistaken human attitude.

This boy must be made to understand that people will attack you even because of the color of your hair! If he managed to understand that he is only the target for something which is always with us, and which is always looking for a target, he would laugh about it and the effect would be that nobody would enjoy attacking him anymore. If we can approach the boy with the methods of Individual Psychology, we will succeed in encouraging him. Then we will even be able to show him that he can become good at arithmetic. There are numerous examples of this. I myself went through this painful experience, and was considered completely inept at arithmetic. I had to repeat a class—and suddenly I was the best mathematician. If my father had followed the advice they gave him at that time, he would have taken me out of school and made me learn a manual trade. I might perhaps have become a good locksmith, but I would have gone through life convinced that there are people who are gifted for arithmetic and others who are not. Having been in that quagmire myself, I can say on very good grounds that I no longer believe this is true.

* 15 *

The Trouble-Maker

Two students, G and S, came for consultation. They are not unusual cases. Rather, they are typical trouble-makers who want to call attention to themselves at any cost, and with whom the teacher has to conduct a futile and exasperating battle.

The one I would like to present first is eight years old; the other is seven. Both of them are in the second grade since one had to repeat a grade. Last year they were in the same class, but had to be separated, since if they had been together they would have made any teaching in the classroom impossible. When separated they are more bearable, although their total absence has a beneficial effect on both the teachers and the class.

In these two boys the cause for being a problem child is different. G is the son of an alcoholic, according to his mother. The father is a teamster, as is one of the brothers, who is seventeen. A second brother, sixteen, runs errands on his motorbike for a baker; and a third brother, fourteen, is an apprentice baker. Also, there is a boy of five—the youngest child in the family. The boy G goes to school in the morning, and to a child care center in the afternoon. He spends all his free time at the stables, or he accompanies teamsters on their rounds. The mother has to work. She is employed by the same baker for whom her sons work. She does not see the boy during the day, since he is not allowed to see her even briefly (probably because the baker is apprehensive of the trouble he might cause). There are a great many disputes and quarrels at home. The mother recognizes the boy's faults—to some extent, at any rate; but she cannot do anything to influence him, since he is the father's favorite; and the father defends him against everyone. The principal means of education in the home are promises of money and monetary rewards. On holidays there is drinking in the home, and the most vulgar popular songs are played on the phonograph—songs that the boy picks up with great enthusiasm. It would seem that on occasion the boy is also taken to bars, where he is served alcoholic beverages. But it is difficult to establish the fact with any certainty, since in what the boy tells he shows great powers of imagination and, on the other hand, the parents deny behaving in this manner. The child also receives money to buy frankfurters at the tavern while his parents go to the movies. At any rate this is how he explains where he got the piece of change which I discovered in his pocket.

His aptitudes are below average. He is not a hard worker. He rarely turns in an assignment. He forgets his notebook; and it does not bother him. At school, the only subjects he participates in voluntarily are drawing and sometimes penmanship. The only thing he really seems to take an interest in is horses. He has never been seriously ill during the school year or in his pre-school period. His attention is distracted by the least little thing. It cannot be established for certain whether he lies deliberately or whether he does it merely in order to give utterance to the things he has imagined. For example, he will say that he went with his father to such and such a place, visited such and such a tavern with him, or spent the night with his aunt, whereas it has been ascertained that he was at home during the time in question. Or, again, he will maintain that in the country he has seen potatoes unearthed with a plow, simply because another boy had told him such a thing. He has absolutely no critical sense. His school work is always disorderly. He is easily influenced in his decisions, and he makes up his mind quickly.

At school he does everything possible to draw attention to himself. He shouts and wrangles during recess, and often during class as well. He hits his schoolmates, and admits he has deliberately tried to hurt them. He pays no attention to scoldings. When he is given a special task to do, he takes advantage of the situation to pick a quarrel or play a silly trick. He often tears up his schoolmates' clothes. Nor does he take care of his own clothes, even if they are new. There was one period when he had to be washed at school. During class he sings. He comments aloud on everything the other children say, and thus interferes with classroom work. He deliberately corrects right answers with wrong ones. He hits his schoolmates who want to answer when called upon. He makes fun of the teacher. If the latter says, "I know who did that," he will shout, "Too bad you really don't!" Outside school he mimics the teacher. He is brutal toward both human beings and animals.

Although he doesn't actually steal, he hides things he finds. It has proven impossible to keep him in the same class with his friend, S. When the teacher made them work in the office, or took them with him into another class when he had to substitute for another teacher, they behaved properly because they apparently lacked a response from the class, or at least familiarity with the students. In any case, the boys behave better when they are separated, when they can't get each other's mutual support. I therefore suggest to see them both together and separated. For the past month, they have been separated. G is in another class, where he is the burden of another teacher. He draws while the others have a discussion or he makes superfluous remarks which cause the whole class to laugh. He uses very vulgar words. As soon as the teacher turns his back, he leaves his seat and picks a quarrel. During recess he has to be isolated; otherwise he hits his schoolmates and kicks them. In the gymnasium he climbs rapidly on the bars and shouts at the same time.

On the subject of this evening's consultation he remarked (in dialect), without of course having been asked about it in the first place: "I know already that the doctor will ask me whether I am a good boy or a bad boy. I'll say I'm a good boy. I don't give a damn. I'm going to bed at five o'clock, and I don't want to be bothered at six-thirty. I'll be sleeping soundly, and they can just try to wake me up. My mother works till nine o'clock at night."

There is a different explanation for S's case. His mother is seriously ill with nephritis, and prior to the child's birth she had been given numerous injections. When he was five years old the boy slid down the banister of the staircase from the third floor of the house to the second floor, and from there he fell. He was taken unconscious to the hospital, where he was under observation for some time, but nothing was discovered.

The mother says that up to the time the boy entered school his father absolutely doted on him. The boy behaved very badly. He would run away and not come home until late at night, and the mother couldn't do anything with him. He often asked her, "When are you going to die? When are you going to the hospital?" After the first complaints from the school, the father became especially severe with him, but without result. The father was a soldier but he is home now. Last year a little girl was born into the family, and this event provoked the boy's jealousy. That same year his tonsils were removed, and he was very ill. He asked, "Why do they vaccinate me and operate on me, and not on my little sister?" When the mother threatens to put him in a corrective institution, he says he would rather be there than at home. His relationship with his uncle and aunt, whom he loves more than his mother, is not very clear. He openly taunts his mother with this. It may be that his aversion against his mother is rooted in this relationship.

During the summer all of the classes spend their recess periods in the park. One day this boy, speaking of an attractive little girl, said, "I'd like to kiss her." The teacher took him aside and asked him in a friendly way why he wanted to do that, and if in general he liked to kiss other people. Finally, he advised him to kiss his mother, but he refused violently. In connection with this matter of kissing, which in itself is a harmless episode, the teacher felt that the boy was badly in want of love at home. He asked the mother to come to school, and suggested that she try to straighten things out by kissing the boy and frequently showing him love, rather than the thrashings she gives him at present. But he encountered indignant resistance. She said that at her house, things weren't done that way.

As for the rest, the boy is very well cared for physically; but he pays no more attention to his belongings than to his school things. The parents are very strict about seeing that he does his assignments. His aptitudes are above average; his attention is easily distracted. He, too, is a careless worker; and he would like to do everything on his own. In general his decisions are easily influenced, and he makes up his mind quickly. During class he interrupts the teacher; pays no heed to remonstration; hits other students for no reason (even when they are not seated near him), throws his books at them, or hits them in the face with his gym shoes. Also, he lies down on his desk, throws chestnuts in the classroom, whistles and sings, and comments on everything said by the teacher or his schoolmates. He picks up colored pencils and claims they are his. When the class does building projects and hangs them on the wall, he takes parts of them down and puts them in his school bag. He often throws down other work baskets; and when he picks them up again, he keeps the scissors.

He performs very poorly the special tasks which are assigned to him as a way of improving his behavior. He uses them only as an opportunity to pick a quarrel or to play tricks. He uses a sponge to splash water on the walls and pictures.

He believes this behavior is heroic. He brags—for example, in telling that when he was at the hospital he avoided getting an injection by running away. His friend G listens to his stories with his mouth agape in admiration. Is S is accused of doing something wrong, he denies it vehemently and may very well say that it is G's fault. Mutual accusations and denunciations are usual with these two boys. S accuses other schoolmates groundlessly, of misdeeds which he invents. His parents' decision to bring him to the guidance center today made him furious at first—especially when he found out that not everyone had to see the doctor.

At school they have already tried everything to change these two boys, with varying success and without permanent improvement. They tried kindly exhortations, promises to satisfy a wish, honorary tasks. They appealed to their honor; painted their prospects for the future, and tried to awaken their compassion. They showed them how painful it would be for them if others behaved as they did. They expelled them from a course they like, gave them individual work in the principal's office, etc. Nothing succeeded. One can sometimes reason with S, but G merely finds it amusing. Up to now the most effective means has been to use "a regular lion tamer's look"; but obviously one can't use this constantly.

Dr. A.: It is certainly not difficult to arrive at a general conclusion as to the excellent report we have on these two boys together, which must be considered not only from the viewpoint of Individual Psychology but also from that of mass psychology. These children know exactly how to respond to any objection, any attack. They seem different when they are elsewhere, but they are always the same. These boys should be removed from the home environment and placed in a special boarding school for a month or two. It seems to me that the time will come that such children who are particularly difficult should be placed in such a home. There, the children would be well treated and we could get a clear picture of them and enlighten them as to the cause of their faults. It is our duty to provide this enlightenment, and I shall try to show you a simplified picture of the type represented by these two boys. In the first case we find an eight-year-old boy, and the most salient facts about him are that he had to repeat a year of school, that he is below average, and whose main interest is in horses.

This boy does not cooperate at school. If we leave aside all other considerations and consider only his behavior, his movements, and his attitude toward the demands of school, we can say that he is in the process of excluding and rejecting all demands. The reason for this is that he does not believe that he can accomplish anything. This motive strikes me as sufficient. Because if I had to identify with this boy and imagine that I could never succeed at anything, but that I was nonetheless compelled to go to school, I would act the same way. Now if we could suddenly capture this boy's attention and explain to him that he could do everything very well that he is wrong in believing that he is good for the stable only and not for school and if we could come to his aid personally and help him succeed, within a reasonable time, in some subjects, we might be able to kindle his interest in school.

We know that his home life, his milieu, is centered on horses, taverns, and pop songs. This environment is not conducive to awakening his interest in school. Someone else has to do this. Now our demand for such a special school emerges again. However, since there is no such school for the boy, the only way he could be helped would be by putting him in care of someone who could give him attention. I am thinking of the function of a kindly older brother who could win the boy over and instill some courage in him. Everything he does at school is an expression of his cowardice, and I would try to explain that to him. I would also like to make him understand that this is why we do not find him on the useful side of life, but elsewhere— on the useless side. I expect a great deal from this explanation. It has large gaps, and it will not be easy to prove this to him. Something is missing upon which we might build.

It must be remembered that he is his father's favorite. This family also seems to offer some good qualities: For example, the children are not badly treated—something one could not say with certainty about the family of the other boy. Yet over-indulgent families like this produce children who immediately try to run away from any difficulty they may encounter. They cannot bear to be in an unfavorable situation. The boy tries everything to make himself appear bigger than he actually is. This boy's striving for recognition, as you can see, takes the center of the stage. It seems to him that the road is blocked for him to gain recognition on the useful side.

It is our duty to confirm the ideas we have set forth. The mother could tell us something about the pampered conditions this boy has been growing up in. I would like to emphasize that the boy is not courageous, and we should ascertain whether this is not manifested in other areas. Perhaps he is afraid of ghosts, afraid to be alone at night and demands that his mother stay with him. Or perhaps he cries out in his sleep. The fact that at school he is arrogant toward his teacher, is not a sign of courage. He knows the limits imposed upon the teacher, and he can behave as if he were a hero.

The second case is a complicated type, more pampered by the father than by the mother. His relationship with his mother is strained, since she has not been able to win his sympathy. On the basis of her reply to the teacher's suggestion that she show the child more love and kiss him sometimes instead of hitting him, we may suppose that the woman is hard and cold. We remember that she replied, "We don't do things that way at my home." In view of her attitude toward the child, it seems likely that more serious things have happened.

This boy has a younger sister. When you hear that a child is more attached to the father than the mother, you can assume that the child is already in the second phase of his development. If for one reason or another the mother has lost contact with the child, the father takes over. Perhaps the father, the aunt, or the uncle gave him more attention because the mother couldn't, owing to her illness. We do not know whether the mother's illness was a sufficient motive for the child's rejection of her.

It may be that the boy had some organic defects. He is more gifted than the average. It is likely that if he were given an intelligence test, his Intelligence Quotient would be high, since his deductive faculties are very good. His behavior at school can be explained from another point of view. He longs for affection. He wants to be pampered. He has experienced what it is to be the center of attention. For six years he was an only child, indulged by everyone, as is always the case with an only child. The aunt and uncle had their share in this. He entered school with the idea that everyone should pay particular attention to him. But this cannot be done at school, because even if one wanted to do it, it would be impossible. Children who always want to draw attention to themselves prefer to make themselves conspicuous in an unpleasant way, on the useless side of life, rather than do it in a pleasant way on the useful side. These pampered children in general are not courageous; they prefer to shine in an easier situation. By comparison with his former situation, this boy feels frustrated both at school and at home. What does a child do when he feels frustrated? When he feels deprived? He tries to enrich himself. It seems apparent to me in his attempts to play the role of the superior person—of the hero. In his fantasy lies we can recognize the same trait. We are not surprised to learn that such children steal. In this boy the point of departure for such an attitude has already manifested itself, since the trifles he steals from his schoolmates represent a desire to enrich himself easily. He behaves like someone whose mode of movement shows that he has the need to possess more—to be more than the others.

The first boy should be encouraged in his studies. The second boy should be made to understand that it is not always necessary to be the center of attention, and that he is not being slighted when people pay attention to someone else. If he wants always to be the center of attention, he must cooperate. If a stranger tells him that, he will think about it. It makes more of an impression. Moreover, the teacher could perhaps give this idea more weight by an understanding smile, as if to say: "You aren't ready yet to bring out in yourself what we are discussing now."

We can find a confirmation of our hypothesis by talking to the child. We are all trying to ascertain whether we are on the right track, or whether we shall have to make corrections. It is very important for us to show this boy a path he can follow, since this is probably more effective and establishes a better social contact than if we punished him. If we make school unpleasant for him by punishment it is possible that he will not go to school any more.

Dr. A. (to the mother of G): The most important thing is to see that this child makes progress. He has lost his courage, he believes he can never become a good student. Does he have any friends?

The mother: He doesn't have any friends in school. He likes to write, but he doesn't like to read. He likes to go to the children's center.

Dr. A.: At the children's center there are no tests and they don't give grades. He must be given some help to make progress—to have success. I wish you would help us in our intention to encourage him. Tell him, "You are an intelligent boy. Don't give up." Is he a nice boy otherwise?

The mother: Yes, but he is wild.

Dr. A.: Do the other children like him?

The mother: He loves to fight with them.

Dr. A.: How does he get along with his father and his brothers? Is he liked in the family?

The mother: They quarrel a lot, like all children.

Dr. A.: Is the father gentle with him?

The mother: My husband loves him very much, and the child is attached to him. As for me, he doesn't obey me unless I give him a talking-to.

Dr. A.: Was he sick when he was little?

The mother: He has a defect in his lungs.

Dr. A.: He must be examined by a doctor, who will certainly give you advice as to his illness. Does he sleep well? Is he restless? Is he afraid of the dark or of ghosts?

The mother: He isn't afraid of anything.

Dr. A.: Let me see him, and we'll find out whether he is timid or not. But don't say anything to him.

(To the audience, after the mother's departure): A child may compensate for his timidity and be arrogant.

(To the child): What do you want to be when you grow up?

G: (no answer).

Dr. A.: What would you like best? Would you like to be an intelligent boy who could do something, or do you believe you will never succeed?

(It is ascertained that he is a left-handed child. This fact must have hindered his progress a great deal.)

You lack courage, and you believe that the others can do everything and you can't do anything. You believe that you will never succeed at anything, and that's why you bother the others. But I had the idea that you were a brave boy. It would be good if you went at your work with courage, and if you paid attention. Things won't go better tomorrow or the day after; but in two weeks you could perhaps become a good student. Everything will go better. What do you say? Do you want to try? Even if you don't get the best grade, you mustn't give up. When you disturb the teacher in class, remember it's because you believe you can't succeed.

(The boy looks at the floor and off to one side.)

When you come back in a month from now, I'll be curious to know whether you already have more courage, or whether you are still a coward.

(The boy, who has not said one word during all this time, goes away.)

Dr. A.: (to the audience): I would like to add one remark. It requires some experience to be able to talk to parents or children. But since this is the case, who could do it if not the teacher himself? It is not merely a question of explaining things in simple words: It is an artistic, dramatic talk we face here. As psychologist and educator, we find ourselves cast in a certain role, and we have no choice but to play this role well and properly, with a definite purpose in mind. You cannot compare this with anything else. We must create an impression, an impression we otherwise find only in art. It is very effective both on adults and children.

(To the mother of S): Are you satisfied with your son?

The mother: He is very bad, very vicious. He bothers the little girl.

Dr. A.: For six years he was the only child. He experienced a tragedy when the little girl was born, because all of a sudden he was no longer the only one. How do you feel about this? Actually, it is quite understandable. We mustn't always be so rigid in our thinking. It is just as though the child suddenly had to leave the warmth and go out into the cold. Was he very attached to you?

The mother: No. Maybe I am too strict.

Dr. A.: It is always difficult for a child when he discovers that there is a difference in the way his parents treat him. It would be good if you could talk to your husband about this, and if you two could equalize your approach.

The mother: I am sick. I have just spent four months in the hospital. I am very nervous. The child never has loved me; he only loves his father.

Dr. A.: Where is the child kept while you are in the hospital?

The mother: Last year I spent six months in the hospital and six months at a resort. My son always stays with his grandmother.

Dr. A.: Grandparents always spoil children. Now he notices the difference. Does he cry out at night? Does he wet the bed?

The mother: He's a little restless. He hasn't been wetting the bed since he was two.

Dr. A.: Does he make friends easily?

The mother: He is very bossy.

Dr. A.: He has the feeling that he is no longer as important as he was at his grandmother's, or he feels that he is being suppressed. For him, obedience means lowering himself. He believes he is suffering an injustice when nobody pays attention to him.

The mother: I always have to talk to him, and he doesn't like me.

Dr. A.: Is he independent when it comes to washing and dressing? Is he sloppy? How about getting up?

The mother: He is sloppy, but he likes to wash himself. He gets up by himself.

Dr. A.: That is very good and very nice. He seems to do good school work. It is only when people don't pay attention to him that he goes wild.

The mother: He always gets on my nerves. Last week he left the house at ten o'clock and promised to get back at noon. But he didn't come back until six o'clock.

Dr. A.: He likes to have people looking for him and worrying about him. Is he brave?

The mother: He isn't afraid of anything.

Dr. A.: I would like to talk to him and tell him that he shouldn't always be playing the big shot. Because if that's the way he behaves at school, he will end up by getting on the wrong track in life. Try to be nicer to him, and tell him gently: "You want me to give all my time to you, but you are already a big boy!"

(The mother leaves.)

Dr. A.: (To the audience): This woman doesn't look particularly sick.

Dr. A.: (To the student, S): How are things in school?

S: Very well.

Dr. A.: Would you like to be the best student? Wouldn't it be fine if you were the best in arithmetic and the best in penmanship; if you could be tops? But for this you have to cooperate. And right now you are refusing to do it most of the time. Don't you want to cooperate? That would really be a lot better.

(It is ascertained that the child is left-handed. Not all children know that they are left-handed, but they experience difficulties.)

How is penmanship going?

S. Not good.

Dr. A.: If you wanted to work hard instead of causing trouble—if you wanted to make an effort—you could write very nicely.

(To the audience): There are two subjects, penmanship and reading, which offer particular difficulties for left-handed children. If you take careful note of the way these children read, you will see that they spell from right to left. This kind of reading doesn't ring true, and one has the impression that they don't know how to read.

(To S): The teacher will have to give you some time and attention. But it isn't fair to bother him in the classroom. What do you gain by that?

S. Nothing at all.

Dr. A.: You could be a good student. Of course it isn't something which is done overnight. But if you try, you can write very nicely. A month from now you can show me how well you are writing. Also, you can tell me if you have enough courage to cooperate. Pay attention to your little sister, and see that your belongings are kept in order. Your mother is sick. She will get well eventually, but you should help her a little.

[The boy leaves.]

I would like to add a few words on the high incidence of left-handed children. There is no such thing as a gifted or an ungifted child. We are discussing two types: the first type, who abandons everything and makes no effort; and the second type, who is always pushing ahead. Some people betray themselves throughout their lives by a certain awkwardness. They don't know that they are left-handed, but they experience the difficulties of left-handedness. Very often they underestimate themselves and overestimate others. You will find a large number of left-handed persons among problem children, neurotics, criminals, potential suicides, and sexual perverts. But you will also find a large percentage of left-handed people among outstanding individuals, among artists, et. al.

Encouragement is the most important factor. If you succeed only in encouraging a student who is left-handed, you will always get good results.

* 16 *

The Struggle for the Lost Paradise

This is a case of a five-year-old pre-school boy whose history will enable us to predict how he will behave at school. I will show you how one can gain clarity and certainty about it, in a very short time.

"This child is difficult to handle."

The child is apparently rebelling. He is living in a state of war and probably in a soft environment, where he is being pampered. Then the question arises: Why is he rebelling at this particular time? Does he feel that he is no longer being pampered as before? At the present time his situation is not so favorable as it was previously. All these things we can predict.

"He is hyperactive."

Is this something new for us? Can we imagine a fighter who is not overactive? If he were not active, we would think he was feeble-minded. These two things are invariably linked in the style of life of the modern child.

"He likes to break things."

This is a way of fighting.

"He sometimes has outbursts of rage."

All these things are not unusual, and the child must be intelligent. We have to ascertain whether he belonged to the category of children who are feeble-minded, and who require a completely different kind of upbringing. Such children have no style of life. This child, on the contrary, has a goal: to fight and win—to have the pleasure, the satisfaction, of being a winner.

"The mother says the child is in good health, and full of life . . . and that he always wants someone to give him personal attention."

This is a struggle which may take place in any family, where the child has to do something to irritate the others.

"He climbs up on the best table in his heavy, dirty shoes. He takes great pleasure in playing with the lamp while his mother is busy."

He knows exactly at what point to make his attack.

"When the mother is going to play the piano, or if she is reading, he chooses that moment to play with the lights. He is never at peace, always restless during meals. He demands constant attention."

He wants to achieve his goal of always being the center of attention. This leads us to the following thought: If he misses so much being the center of attention, it indicates that he has been there in the past, and that he wants to restore this situation. What event aggravated his situation so much? Perhaps it is a younger child.

"He is always boxing with his father, and he wants to play with him."

We can see that he always finds a way to fight and to cause trouble.

"He has the habit of plunging his hand into a cake and then stuffing his mouth full of it."

He could also show his rebellion by refusing to eat.

"If the mother has guests, he pushes them out of their chairs, and sits down in their place."

This act proves that he doesn't like others. Here we see a lack of social feeling, which explains his bad humor toward his little brother.

"When the mother and father sing or play the piano, the child shouts constantly and says he doesn't like it."

This doesn't suit him. He wants people to give their time exclusively to him. But when we see a fault, we should not punish. Punishing is of no help. We know where we must begin. This boy feels offended, injured, relegated to the background.

"The father is a singer, and gives concerts. The mother accompanies him. The little boy cries loudly: 'Daddy, come here!' "

Thus we see that all of his efforts are aimed at keeping the father and mother occupied with him personally.

"He has fits of anger if he wants something and doesn't get it immediately."

This is his fighting attitude.

"He destroys everything. With a screwdriver, he removes all the screws from his bed."

Here his asocial attitude appears once again. He does everything he can to bother his parents and show his bad humor.

"He makes cynical remarks to people, especially when he has done something wrong and knows that he can get away with it. People consider him to be an intelligent boy because he makes caustic remarks. He cannot keep himself occupied with one thing for any length of time. His mother tries to keep him occupied." (Obviously, she does not succeed.)

"When the mother slaps him, he laughs and is quiet for perhaps two minutes. The mother thinks that she, the father and grandmother have pampered the child excessively. At present, to tell the truth, he is no longer pampered."

He has become the way he is because his social feeling could not develop, since he has been close only to his mother and father.

"The father and mother are always exhausted, but the boy never is."

It is understandable that he doesn't tire when playing a game which pleases him. The job of working with the boy doesn't please either the mother or the father; thus they grow weary. Constraint serves no purpose, since he takes vengeance when someone constrains him.

"He has no memory, and he cannot concentrate."

This is because he does not have the necessary equipment and preparation for it. He should be able to function independently, but he can't.

"He has never been to kindergarten."

It would appear, then, that the mother raised him only for herself.

It is very important how we interpret these relationships. We can speak of understanding when we know that we are dealing here with only a part of the whole. This is not a physiological process. To understand means to grasp the relationship of all things.

* 17 *

Stealing Because of Lost Affection

"The child was born in a village in the southern part of Hungary."

"When the child was two and one-half years old, his father's business went bankrupt."

This already gives us something to think about. Until his third year the child probably enjoyed a favorable material situation, which must have changed thereafter and for the worse. Through his father's business failure, the child's situation became more difficult by which he became over-burdened. It is not easy to adapt from a favorable to an unfavorable situation. Children who have enjoyed a good material situation in the early part of their lives are always affected if a change takes place later.

"With his wife and his only child, he moved to Vienna to look for work."

We learn now that at the time the boy was an only child, pampered, and used to being the center of attention. We can predict that a new and unfavorable situation put a heavy pressure on the boy.

"During the next seven years the father made his living as a travelling salesman. . . ."

This fact is important. We have often found in such cases that the mother—due to the father's frequent absences—cannot fulfill her second function; namely, to guide the child's social interest toward other persons, and particularly toward the father. This is generally true when the father is seldom at home. The mother cannot perform her second function. This is also applicable where there is serious disagreements in a marriage. In this case, too, it is impossible to awaken the child's interest in others. Children of unhappy marriages often become problem children. Also, a father's fits of anger, or a tyrannical upbringing hinder the development of the social sense.

". . . and fought through a lawsuit which had ensued upon his business failure."

If we try to identify with the child's situation, we can understand that the whole atmosphere in which the child lived was depressed by this lawsuit alone.

Whether the atmosphere in the home had a strong impact on the child cannot be ascertained."

It is likely that even though nothing of this atmosphere remained in the child's memory, it influenced his style of life.

"In any case, he used to be an obedient, quiet, and sweet child...."

Which means to us that he was very attached to his mother.

"... attached by a great love to his mother, who was very young but not always very just, and even more to his father, who was gentle and good."

If this observation is accurate, we must emphasize the expression "not always very just." It is likely that since the mother was not able to fulfill her first function properly, the child sought another person. Despite his frequent absences from home, the father was able to win the affection of the child, who in his second phase became attached to him.

"In the spring the family moved, and the father started a small business for the mother and one of his younger brothers."

We interpret this fact as follows. Since the mother was undertaking a new occupation, the situation deteriorated for the child, because the mother now no longer had so much time to pamper him and make him the center of attention.

"It is likely that the child has been in bad company."

This information confirms our hypothesis that the mother did not have much time any more to devote to the child, who always wanted someone near him.

"He stole neckties from his parents' shop...."

This child probably had the feeling that he had been robbed of something. The father travels, the mother is at the store, and the child has no one to care for him. This gives him the feeling of being deprived. We are going to find out what he did with the neckties. Perhaps he gave them to other children in order to win their affection and warmth—something which he can no longer get from his mother.

"... in order to give them to the apprentice painter who lived in the building."

This strongly confirms our theory.

"He stole roses from a nearby park, either to bring them home or to give them to a very pretty aunt whom he loved very much."

Like many children who feel they have been robbed of something, he has begun to bribe others with gifts to win their love and affection. This is one of the commonest motives for theft among children.

It is a motive which is completely disregarded by the Juvenile Court, for example, where no one is concerned with this point of view.

"One day, when the boy was eight years old, he was leaving school with his friends when they met the priest. The other boys greeted the priest politely, but the boy shouted obscenities at him."

So he is a freethinker! We must go further with our deductions. This boy who wants so badly to be the center of attention probably has a strong urge to make himself noticed. Since is seems hopeless to him to achieve this by useful action, he tries another way.

"Why did he do this?" asked the person who drew up this report.

"He had never had anything to do with this priest. What was the motive for his bad behavior?"

Perhaps he belonged to another denomination.

"An hour later he was taken to the school to kiss the priest's hand and ask his pardon, but he refused.

Here again you have the image of his whole character. This boy, who has always wanted to play a dominating role, is unwilling to yield to anyone. He doesn't want to acknowledge his guilt. We are not inclined to demand of children that they apologize or acknowledge their guilt. We would prefer to handle the matter somewhat along the lines which I once experienced. At the age of six, I once did something wrong. My mother, her face red with anger, demanded an explanation. I was very embarrassed since I was aware of my guilt. My father, who had been standing near her without saying anything, finally took her by the hand and said to her: "Let him go." This scene made a strong impression on me, and I have always remembered it. I am most grateful to my father for this. It influenced me more positively than if I had had to do penance, or if my mother had given me a slap. Forcing a child to apologize is not a good method. There is no doubt that this boy knew he had behaved badly. Why demand a public confession from him? Why humble him in public, and show that he had to submit?

"He received a bad mark in conduct, and for the rest of the year he had to sit in the last row."

We can predict that this measure will likewise fail to have a good effect on him, since in this way, too, he remains the center of attention. He will create disturbances, make himself conspicuous in an unpleasant manner, and will behave like a hero.

"The teacher, however, did not treat him badly."

Here, certainly, we have an attenuating factor which will probably bear good fruit. If the teacher had shown a hostile attitude, the boy would have rebelled even more.

"A small incident which occurred during that period, left an indelible impression on his memory. One day when he was walking in the courtyard, he gave to a workman who was doing a job there, a piece of unleavened bread he was eating. The workman put the piece of bread on his workbench and smashed it into crumbs with his hammer, saying: "This is the way we ought to crush all Jews.'

As we can see, he is a Jewish boy. It is natural that this remark weighed heavily on this child who is looking for affection and gentleness. As an adult, we might perhaps laugh about this. We would recognize this incident as part of a general climate, and if we want to explore this question, we would look instead for the roots of this feeling. As far as the boy is concerned we shall see whether this incident had other consequences.

"Is it not possible to ascertain whether this incident took place before or after the incident with the priest."

It would have been interesting and important to ascertain this point. It is possible that this incident unleashed a hostile attitude in him, and that the insult to the priest was a result of his hostile attitude.

"In the spring of the following year the father closed up the business and the little family moved again back into the city. At the end of the year or early the following spring the father had to start serving the prison term to which he had been sentenced for his fraudulent bankruptcy.

Again a new impression on the soul of this child who is eager for affection, and very much attached to his mother. He experiences that his gentle father is sent to prison. I would not be surprised if the child rebelled violently against our laws and challenged the entire society. Perhaps it will become apparent that he cannot develop an interest in others, that he even loses any remnant of social feeling. He may join forces with other asocial elements or find his own way toward crime.

"No one ever talked to the child about this event."

It is extremely difficult to hide such an event from a child. Obviously, it would have been much better if he had never been informed of his father's prison term. But we doubt that this was possible in this case.

"Later, as an adolescent and an adult, he avoided starting any discussion on this subject."

He regarded it as a deep humiliation.

"He always pretended to be ignorant of the event, and never talked about it—even to his most intimate friends."

This fact is very interesting, since if the boy had rebelled and had regarded it as an injustice, he would justifiably have insisted on pointing out the plight of his poor father. There must have been a very strong streak of middle-class tradition and thinking in the boy to make it impossible for him to talk about it openly and freely. One cannot talk about everything, there are things which just can't be discussed. In this boy, who in a moment of rebellion is beginning to leave the framework of society, we can already discover a certain insecurity in his attitude. External events are extremely meaningful. It is possible that he would have led a decent life if his father had not been sent to prison, and if he had not felt oppressed because of his religion.

"Suddenly the wildness of the past two years disappeared. The boy turned with increased tenderness toward his young, pretty mother, and became obedient and quiet."

Here we see a manifestation of his need to be close to someone— not a large group of people, but one person alone. He is used to attaching himself to one person alone. If his father is taken away from him for a while, he looks for someone else. When his mother was busy, he tried to win the sympathy of the apprentices. He always needs someone to be close to.

"After the father was discharged from prison he was able, by constant work, to overcome the material difficulties caused by his absence. It seemed that a prolonged pressure had been lifted from the family."

Because of the financial difficulties, the boy once again had felt the pressure of external circumstances.

"The child recovered his animation."

We are still not satisfied, since we do not know what this means nor why it happened. The boy does not yet know what his attitude should be, since he remembers his father from the past as someone who pampered him.

"During his first year of school he was among the best students. After that, he dropped down below the average. Now in the second term of the fifth grade he is lively and full of good spirits."

This corresponds to the time when his father returned.

"He is nevertheless obedient and a hard worker. He soon became one of the best students in his class."

It is likely that he had a teacher who sympathized with him.

"The teacher, whom he admired a great deal, praised him on several occasions for this improvement; and this praise was good for him."

Once again he found someone who paid attention to him. He seems to have been saved by the love and affection given to him.

"In the fall he made a good start in secondary school."

Our only apprehension is: What will happen if he cannot secure for himself, at school, a situation wherein he is appreciated? It could be that he might get a teacher whom he doesn't like, or that he will have trouble because of his religion and feel that he is being rejected. Perhaps he will encounter difficulties in a certain subject, or will not be able to find an adequate method for his work. Also, later in life he may encounter situations in which warmth is lacking. Such are our reservations so far as his future development is concerned.

"In November the father was brought home seriously ill."

Here again our experience comes to our assistance. It tells us that if such a child loses contact because of the illness of one of the parents who has pampered him—the father's illness takes almost all of the mother's time—and no longer has the feeling of rapport he used to have, it is a new, and often a very difficult situation. In such situations setbacks become apparent. This is something we can easily imagine. The father is brought home seriously ill; the mother must care for him; and once again, the child is left alone. If he had the good fortune at this time to get a teacher who would give him time and attention, this difficulty might disappear. But for the moment we have no information on this point.

"During his return trip the father, who was then forty years old, had a stroke and became paralyzed on the left side of his body."

We can understand what it means to a family when the head of the household, the breadwinner, falls seriously ill—especially when the family is a close one, as this family certainly was. We can also imagine the consequences of this event.

"His business failure had resulted from the numerous financial sacrifices he had had to make for his parents and his younger brothers and sisters, of whom there were several."

This is something which the boy probably knew too, and which gave him the impression that the father was a just and honest man.

"The physical breakdown of this man, who up to that time had been perfectly healthy, must certainly have been due to the nervous strain of the lawsuit (which dragged on for several years); his regrets that he could no longer help his parents, brothers, and sisters; overwork and anxiety; and the unfortunate circumstance that he could not unburden himself to anyone—not even to his wife (whom, incidentally, he indulged a great deal)."

Here the report ends, and we are left with our speculations. If the boy feels at ease at school he will overcome his difficulties. If he is taken out of school he will have to bow to his fate and content himself with an inferior job—a situation which will cause him great suffering. We know that he has an automatic style of life which is manifested by his need to find someone to whom he can be very close. If he comes to feel that he is rejected, or if he is disturbed by his strong feeling of inferiority, we should not be surprised to see a recurrence of something we have observed already: his vigorous rebellion. If he finds a favorable situation in which someone gives him time and attention, this boy may very well go through life without giving anyone grounds for reproval.

Later on, he will perhaps make satisfactory progress. In the exercise of his occupation he will not encounter any particular difficulties if he is in a situation which suits him. Solving the problem of love will be more difficult for him, since he will always look for someone who will pamper him. In life he will always look for a woman who will behave somewhat like his mother, in whom he found everything he desired, as we have ascertained. But this situation could come about only by a happy coincidence.

I am not displeased at having had to exert myself on a fragmentary report and to have tested our knowledge on it. In this connection I would like to note that it is much less important to know whether we have surmised correctly everything which might take place later on. It suffices for us to have exerted ourselves on a fragmentary report and to have emphasized details more precisely than is usually the case. The same thing holds true in life, when we meet persons about whom we have only fragmentary knowledge so that we must divine the rest. It is not our lot to find finished portraits: we must always draw the conclusions ourselves. This has to be done with some caution and with the thought in mind that the further development of the child will offer us further clues.

* **18** *

The Bed-Wetter

"Emil is twelve years old and suffers from enuresis."

When we hear of a case of enuresis we can assume, on the basis of our experience, that it involves a movement which has the goal of establishing contact with the mother, although in an improper fashion. The boy in question expresses himself through his enuresis. It is just as though he were speaking "bladder lingo." We can consider all of a patient's forms of expression as varieties of language. Here the language means: "I am not far enough advanced yet. I still have to be watched over!" And usually the mother gets up two or three times a night to watch over the child and to awaken him. The child gives his mother extra work.

Enuresis is not an organic disease; and we know that an enuretic child is quite capable of controlling his bladder during the day. The problem is to find out why he cannot control it during the night. The reason is that he is under psychic tension which makes it impossible for him to hold back his urine. Where does this tension come from? We know how stubbornly children persist in their wetting. They are seeking a contact; they want to be close to someone —to give extra work to someone. (Remark made by a patient: ".They want to establish a kind of branch with somebody.") This is the type of the pampered child. When we see such an effort to be pampered even more, we know that the child has been having some difficulty in maintaining his contact. We already have enough knowledge to be able to say that enuresis is apparently a form of attack resulting from a rebellious attitude adopted by a child to gain attachment. This type also includes children who are constantly restless in their sleep, who cry out at night *(pavor nocturnus)*, and who try to make contact with others by means of noise. There are also children who get up and walk about in order to establish contact by movement, and thereby provoke others to pay attention to them. This is language expressed by another organ. It is significant to see how the child manages to express it. It is connected with an organic inferiority of the bladder and the nervous centers which control the bladder. I was the first (in 1907) to point out that enuretics have a weakness of the lumbar segment. I have also emphasized that there is a connection between enuresis and the spina bifida or a nerve in that region. (Professor Fuchs has stressed this.) Also, we must understand how the child speaks this "bladder language." It is found chiefly in children whose attention has been drawn to the importance of the function, and where the mother has made a special effort to keep the child dry at night, where she has overemphasized this cleanliness. Thus the child automatically arrives at the idea: Something can be done here; this is a point of attack. You will see that in all these children one always finds the symptoms of pampering.

We don't want to be dogmatic, so let us see what the rest of the report says.

He is twelve years old. We must keep in mind the fact that he has been pampered, and that since the bed-wetting persists he has the impression that he is not getting enough love. We can deduce certain details from this. He probably has a younger brother or sister. These are the pampered child's motives for launching an attack; or it is an accusation that he is now being less pampered. An accusation is identical with an attack. There is no difference. He has been dislodged from his position. Perhaps he has a stepfather or stepmother. We have no fixed rule to go by. But it is very important for us to know what is taking place. We must find out why this child is less pampered now than before. The boy has a fictitious ideal (his ideal is his goal): to be pampered; to have someone at his beck and call. We must change this goal and show him another one, so that he can make himself useful.

"Never at night; only in the daytime."

This information influences our thinking very strongly. During the day he is under great tension; at night he seems to be content. One can imagine all sorts of things and assume that he often sleeps with his mother at night, whereas during the day he wants to make himself conspicuous in an unpleasant way, as if he were saying: "You must give me more personal attention." During the day his struggle is more intense.

"He often loses control of his bowels."

For the same reason he makes himself conspicuous by having a bowel movement in his pants. He is struggling under conditions of complete discouragement. Whether one should diagnose imbecility in this case depends upon how one interprets this definition. We ask: Why doesn't he do it at night? We sometimes find that children who become deeply involved in their games, lose all control of their functions. On the basis of these details we can assume that here we are dealing with a social function. A function which is fulfilled outside of any social behavior pattern must be considered abnormal.

"He is an illegitimate child."

We may assume that such children have been reared without love, without the warmth of affection, and without that atmosphere of tenderness which is usually created around children during the first few years of their lives. But we also find pampered children among illegitimates. Hence we must obtain more information on the subject.

"His father was killed in the war, and his mother remarried."

Our hypothesis as to a stepfather is confirmed.

"Two children have been born of this second union: a boy eight years old and a girl of six."

If you will remember that I was previously talking about an accusation, you will see that our interpretation of the case was accurate. He is probably right in making his accusation, and there is no doubt that he feels he is right. I remember a case in which a little boy had lost his mother when he was two weeks old. The father remarried a short time later, and no one knew that the child did not belong to the new mother. No one had ever told him. Later on another child was born. When the boy came to me for consultation subsequently, he told me that until the age of fourteen he had been convinced that the woman was not his mother, but a stepmother, and that this impression was then confirmed. This incident proves to what extent children distinctly feel these details, even when they are well treated. They notice a difference nonetheless. When there are other children, they feel that the latter are given more attention and more care.

"The child's behavior toward his brother and sister is supposedly very good."

We don't see any struggle among these children. I have often found that a child can love his brothers and sisters even though he is jealous. He may feel at a disadvantage, but he can get along with them. A feeling of this kind may have various results. To cite an example: A girl of five, who had been the only child up until that time, had a little sister. Later on it was learned that this older girl had killed three little girls, as if she wanted to say: "All girls must disappear." And yet she had behaved impeccably toward her younger sister. She had carried out her murders with great skill, and she was not caught until the third one.

"The stepfather was very severe with him at first."

The boy went through a sad period. When the stepfather came upon the scene his situation deteriorated, and it was then that his accusations began.

"But thanks to the mother's intervention the situation improved."

We can imagine that the improvement was not great enough for the boy to feel it permanently.

"During most of his childhood the boy has been far from home. either at his aunt's house. . . .

This happened probably during the first part of his life. He must have experienced better days there. Generally, children are well treated when they stay with their aunts or grandmothers.

". . . or at the orphans' home."

I will not affirm that he was well treated at that institution. My impressions of these homes are not the best. They have a strict discipline, and it is part of this discipline that children do not wet their pants or dirty themselves. You can see that in this area there was an overemphasis for the child. It is also likely that the aunt overstressed the importance of these functions. We can observe that if a child is particularly admonished about the importance of eating, the child will prove difficult in this area. Also, children who want to acquire the mastery over their limbs and their bodily functions, refuse to take orders on this subject. You will find that such children may get up at night, half-asleep, and perform their function on the toilet without assistance. But when they awaken and someone wants to take them to the toilet, they refuse and scream with rage.

We do not have enough information to know where the mistake in this boy's upbringing was made. It is likely that he had to change from a favorable situation to an unfavorable one.

"The boy now goes to the first grade of secondary school."

I believe he is a little behind for his age. He should have been in this grade at the age of ten or eleven. You can however be sure that since he has been able to come this far and go to secondary school, he is neither an idiot nor an imbecile nor feeble. It is likely that he would have been a better student if he had not been constantly suffering from psychic tension.

"He had to repeat the first and third grades of primary school."

This corroborates our hypotheses that he suffered from tension and was not adequately prepared, especially for a strict teacher. He took one more step toward hopelessness. Also, these occurences must have been detrimental to his situation at home.

"Now he is making satisfactory progress at school."

It is likely that the teacher is kind.

"He has friends."

He is beginning to regain hope and look at life with more courage.

"He often makes faces, in school or outside."

These grimaces, too, are again a form of expression which we may consider a language. What is his purpose? He says: "Look at me!" He is playing a role, a comedy, in order to attract the attention of others. Here we have the same phenomenon we find in his wetting and dirtying himself. He would like to move further into the foreground. He has the impression that he is being pushed into the background and fights against it.

"Supposedly, he began to walk at the age of eleven months, and didn't begin to talk until rather late."

There are children in whom the development of language follows external circumstances (mutism). We could have understood it if someone had maintained that this boy is an imbecile, although such is not the case.

"Also, he shows a speech defect. When he talks, he pushes his tongue between his teeth."

This is what we call "lisping." I do not understand why people don't correct this defect. This boy should be shown in a friendly manner how to hold his tongue when talking, or one could employ some wire devices. It is relatively easy to correct this defect—which, in this case, must have contributed even more to make him feel his role was unpleasant. No doubt he has been teased, and this must have discouraged him.

"It seems that the father had the same speech defect."

It is not the speech defect which is transmitted, but perhaps the form of the tongue or the conformation of the jaw. All speech defects are influenced by special organic conditions. In stutterers we often find either an abnormal arrangement of the bony frame of the jaw or larynx, or dental anomalies. All these factors tend to hinder the normal development of pronunciation, and facilitate a speech defect.

"Childhood diseases: measles, chicken-pox, plus pneumonia. Removal of adenoids and tonsils three years ago."

We cannot make much use of this information.

"The child is fragile and asthenic, and gives the impression of timidity and fright."

We did not expect the child to give an impression of courage. He had reached a state of discouragement. If he has slightly improved recently, it is perhaps because he has made progress at school.

"Owing to the fact that his upper jaw overrides his lower one strongly, and that he almost constantly keeps his mouth open, he gives an impression of stupidity."

You can see that he has an abnormal jaw structure. His stupid appearance must have contributed to the fact that he is disliked.

"Organic examination: nothing noteworthy; reflexes normal; neurological examination not made; examination of nose and pharynx likewise not yet made. The mother and one brother had nephritis."

From the viewpoint of Individual Psychology it is very interesting that in enuretics one finds an imperfection of the entire urogenital system (for example, imperfection of a kidney)—a fact I have already emphasized in my study on "organ inferiority." These imperfections sometimes give a basis for diseases; but this does not mean that enuresis is itself the consequence of an organic disease. There exists an embryonic inferiority which favors the development of enuresis. Enuretics also manifest a weakness of the digestive tract and of the genital organs. The weakness of the genital organs is present in almost all cases.

We must now find how we can talk to the mother and ascertain whether this child's case is really so desperate. Also, we will try to see whether the boy has not improved recently, since we have noticed such favorable signs as the fact that he has friends and is doing better at school. We must also influence the mother to make the boy understand his own value, and to show him that he is not being rejected. We should urge her to persuade the father to be friendly to the boy, to give him a little pleasure from time to time, such as taking him alone for a walk on Sunday. If these things are done the boy will abandon his attitude of accusation and stop spoiling the pleasures of the family.

We must encourage the boy himself so that he can have some success. Also, we should propose a goal for him, making sure that it is one he can achieve. We will try to give him the task to find out if he is capable of establishing friendly relations with his parents. If we succeeded here in creating in him a friendlier attitude, he himself will make an effort to avoid annoying others. It may be supposed that he does not dirty his pants at school. He does it only where he feels completely discouraged.

You can perceive the most important points: to persuade the parents to take a more favorable attitude toward the child; to encourage the boy, and make him understand the importance of an occupation.

Dr. A. (to the mother): We would like to talk to you about your boy. How is he doing at school?

The mother: He has been trying hard lately.

Dr. A.: Has he already said what he would like to be in life?

The mother: He'd like to be an electrician.

Dr. A.: He already has ambition? Does he understand anything about this kind of work?

The mother: Yes, he shows some understanding of it.

Dr. A.: Does he make himself useful around the house?

The mother: Yes.

Dr. A.: Is he happy when his services are recognized and he is praised for them? I would like to see this child praised a good deal. He has a great need for praise. He would like to be treated with tenderness and gentleness. How does he get along with you?

The mother: He obeys. I can count on him.

Dr. A.: Does he take care of the other children? Does he get along with them?

The mother: The second child doesn't let him tell him what to do.

Dr. A.: The second child is always more lively and faster. Second children always move more rapidly. How does he sleep?

The mother: He snores very loud. He had adenoids.

Dr. A.: Where does he sleep?

The mother: He sleeps in my room. I think my son is afraid of my second husband, and he is afraid of everything. He used to be with strangers. His aunt was very good to him; then he went to the orphanage.

Dr. A.: *(His change of situation began at the orphanage.)* Couldn't you convince your husband that he should behave so that the child will no longer be afraid of him? He is a nice boy, and he needs to be treated with tenderness and kindness. Something good can be made out of him. If your husband would take him for walks on Sunday and give him some pleasure, it would be a very good thing. You must never beat the boy or shout at him. He is on a very good track, and he will develop well. What position does he sleep in at night?

The mother: He sleeps on his stomach.

Dr. A.: *(He is turning away from life and hiding.)*

The mother: He puts the covers over his head. Ever since he came back from the orphans' home he has been afraid.

Dr. A.: Try for once not to criticize him or scold him. I would tell him: "You are a capable boy!" I would praise him and show him that I love him. A child like this needs proof of affection. If you did this, everything would go better with him. Doesn't he want to leave you?

The mother: When I tell him I'll make him go back to the orphans' home, he is afraid.

Dr. A.: I wouldn't tell him a thing like that. Is he the same at school and at home?

The mother: At school he is afraid because he can't leave the class all the time. When he has to go, he is afraid to ask the teacher.

Dr. A.: It might be a good idea to warn the teacher by means of a note from the hospital. (The mother leaves.)

Dr. A. (to the boy): Hello, there! How are you doing at school? What would you like to become?

Emil: A mechanic.

Dr. A.: Good! Are you capable? How is your penmanship coming along?

Emil: Not good.

Dr. A.: And drawing?

Emil: Pretty good.

Dr. A.: You can become a good mechanic, but you must have courage. You must not be afraid. Nobody has anything against you. Do you want to learn how not to be afraid? You don't have to behave like a baby in front of the teacher. You are already a big boy; you're not a baby any more. Even when you get a bad mark, you shouldn't be afraid. I had bad grades once, too. But then I went at my lessons harder, and things went better. You mustn't always be afraid. When you are afraid, you behave like a baby. How much longer do you have to go to school?

Emil: Two years more. Then I can become an apprentice.

Dr. A.: How about gymnastics? How are things going there?

Emil: I got a B!

Dr. A.: Do you have many friends?

Emil: I have some bad friends, too. They always beat me.

Dr. A.: Do you fight with them?

Emil: Sometimes.

Dr. A.: You mustn't hurt others. It's something like an exercise in gymnastics. Do you fight with your brother, too?

Emil: He's eight years old.

Dr. A.: Then you're the oldest one. Is he nice?

Emil: He is bad, too, and he picks fights with me.

Dr. A.: He doesn't seem to be so afraid. You must try to make progress. If he can behave like a grown-up when he is only eight, you must try to do it, too. Come back in a month and tell me how you are—if you have more courage and are behaving like a grown-up and not like a baby any more. Try it, and then tell me if you have been able to do it. (The child leaves.)

For the time being, all we can do is encourage him. If we talk to him about his faults, we won't encourage him. If he comes back in a month and we can see that he is making progress, we can then go into the question of his faults.

* **19** *

Enuresis: A Means of Attachment

"F, who is twelve years old, comes to the clinic because of enuresis."

This is a rebellious child. Probably he was pampered at one time and something has changed that favorable situation. Now he does not feel well and has begun to attack his mother so that she has to look after him also at night. We must seek for indications that he is in fact a pampered child; i.e., whether he is generally sloppy, probably jealous of a younger child, troublesome at mealtime, whether he tries to be the center of attention or tries to win the sympathy of others.

"He often wets himself in the daytime. . . ."

If you hear of a child wetting himself in the daytime, it is an indication of a battle which has already become very violent. He is not content to disturb others at night, but does it in the daytime as well. We must also ascertain whether he does not present some mental deficiencies. Organic diseases which cause this kind of enuresis are rare.

". . . but only rarely at night."

During the daytime he carries on a violent battle. At night he is probably in a more favorable situation, and he quiets down. We should not be surprised if we were told that he carries on this struggle consciously, and that his dominant character trait is stubbornness. Because stubbornnesss represent a more conscious rebellion.

"When his mother is with him, or when he is at school, he never wets himself."

This indicates that his enuresis is motivated by psychic factors. When his mother is near him he does not have to try to attract her to him. It is likely that he also feels at ease in school. Perhaps he is a good student. Or perhaps he wants to avoid being expelled from school.

"The mother is divorced."

The break-up of a marriage has a very bad influence on children. Usually, couples who quarrel pay little attention to their children, and are ill-tempered toward them. It should be noted that the children of unhappy or bad marriages are often found among problem children, delinquents, neurotics, sexual perverts, and drunkards. We shall try to see whether this child was not overburdened, since this is always an aggravating factor.

"He lives with his grandparents."

It must be remembered that grandparents usually pamper their grandchildren. Not always, however; if the mother spoils the child, the grandmother reproaches her for it. But if the mother does not spoil the child, the grandmother does.

"The child used to sleep in his parents' bedroom."

This proves that the child was spoiled at one time either because he was able to get close to his mother through his own efforts or because the parents always wanted to have him with them.

"Now he sleeps alone."

This fact is not without its importance for us; and it certainly plays a role in the boy's enuresis. If the child were sleeping in his mother's bed he would not wet himself.

"The child is strongly attached to his mother."

This confirms that the child is closely tied to his mother. He tries to win over his mother and use her as a support.

"He is very pampered by his grandparents."

Thus our suppositions are confirmed.

"Four years ago he was in th hospital for seven months with oste-omyelitis of the hip and femur."

This is a disease which tends to increase pampering. It is one of the typical events after which the child will miss very strongly the pampering which was given to him during his illness. A child is never so pampered as when he is hospitalized with osteomyelitis.

"At the time an amputation was being considered. However, the boy was cured—but he was left with badly stiffened joints."

Thus he has an organic defect. This circumstance tends to awaken and maintain in children a strong feeling of inferiority. Pampered children have an *a priori* feeling of inferiority; they doubt their own ability. Because of the fact that this boy has ankylosis, his feeling of inferiority is intensified: he tries to lean on others even more.

"Because of this illness he missed school from the age of seven to ten."

Evidently he spent those years close to his mother.

"When he was ten years old he entered the third grade in the special remedial school. Now he is in the fourth grade of that school."

Remedial school represents a further accentuation of inferiority. Only if the child is an imbecile, an idiot or a moron will he not notice that he is among backward children. In Vienna, for example, it is a common practice to speak of "idiot classes" in such a case. A normal child has a feeling of degradation if through mischance he is put into a remedial school. Thus this child has several motives for feeling inferior and discriminated against.

"He does good work at school."

We are not surprised to learn that he is making good progress at school, if he is mentally normal. This is not an advantage; to be one-eyed among the blind is no triumph.

"He has trouble with arithmetic."

If eventually he finds the right method for doing arithmetic, he will be able to do arithmetic as well as the others.

"If the teacher calls upon the other students, he answers aloud."

We can conclude from this that he is an intelligent boy. This pampered child would like to put himself into the foreground. His bed-wetting is another means of achieving this. At school he plays a pretty good role—he does not have to be dissatisfied with himself. But even there he would like to get ahead of the others, and this is why he always raises his voice.

"Even when he is playing with the other children he must always play the leading role."

He has his own style—something you will not find in feeble-minded children. We can say that he does not belong in the remedial school. We know that because of his illness he was adequately prepared for regular class, and that it would be difficult for him to keep up. A special preparatory school should be established for students like this one.

"He has a brother, four and one-half years older than he, who at one time was very pampered by his father."

We conclude from this that he has no younger brothers or sisters. He no doubt has a firm conviction that the older brother is ahead of him. The latter has been pampered by the father, and he is not in a remedial school.

"The older brother is very handsome. He had to repeat the first year of secondary school, but now he does very good work. He is a serious student and very adult."

When we hear of two brothers, where the older one is developing well and is unbeatable, the younger boy is usually a problem child. If it is the younger one who makes good progress and follows his older brother easily, or even threatens his position, it is the older one who will become a problem child. This theory is confirmed once again in this case. It is likely that the older brother does not have any qualms about remarking that his brother is in the remedial school.

"The boy is very fond of playing the clown."

This is a frequent manifestation in children with a strong feeling of inferiority, who do nothing, and want to be the center of attention. We often find three coordinated manifestations in such children: enuresis, the need to interrupt others, and clowning. They are all forms of expression employed by an ambitious weakling. A person who has confidence in himself does not behave like this.

"He often cries out at night."

Here, again, he is seeking contact. The fact that he screams at night and clowns is proof of his intelligence. He does everything the right way; just the way we would do them (if I may say so) if we were in the same situation, and if we misinterpreted this situation, which actually demands courage from us.

"At mealtime he does not cause any trouble about eating."

This is a sign that this family has not made any severe mistakes in the boy's training, that they have not overstressed the importance of food. It was the boy who made a mistake here: he should have created difficulties about eating, too. We shall not be surprised, however, if his style of life fails to exhibit certain symptoms which we might have expected to find on the basis of our greater experience.

"He washes and dresses himself without any assistance."

In this area, too, he has probably had proper training.

"The parents are grandparents on his father's side and are blood relatives."

Basically, this is of no importance, since the same symptoms can be observed in other children. His failures cannot be attributed to hereditary factors. But I would like to emphasize that I have always found a lack of courage in those who contract consanguineous marriages. They are seeking a kind of security in their choice of partner; and they tend to find it in persons whom they have known since childhood. It also indicates a weak social feeling, since for them their family represents all of society. It cannot be denied that marriages between blood relatives sometimes produce children with organic inferiorities (impaired hearing or eyesight). But from what I have been able to ascertain so far, this happens only in cases where both partners had identical organic inferiorities. In the case of consanguineous marriages where these parellel weaknesses do not exist, we find often perfectly healthy children. I am opposed to marriages between blood relatives only because the social feeling demands the mixing of blood on the widest basis. Individuals who find a great difference between those of their own family and others do not have much social feeling.

"The child has had chicken-pox and whooping-cough."

Parents pamper children a good deal while they are going through these diseases. You will observe that there is a series of children's diseases which automatically cause parents to pamper their children. Examples of such diseases are scarlet fever and whooping-cough. There we subsequently find a series of difficulties, which can be attributed to these diseases. On the other hand, you will sometimes observe that a problem child improves after a serious illness. However, we won't go so far as to say that scarlet fever could have a favorable influence on a child's character.

"He learned to walk at the age of sixteen months."

If the mother is not mistaken, the child may have been somewhat rachitic. It is obvious that the mother watched over him more closely than was necessary.

"He did not learn to speak correctly until the age of three."

This proves that he was not particularly in need of language. Because if language had been necessary to him he would have learned to talk sooner. Everything was done for him, all his wishes fulfilled, without him having to talk. The same thing is found in mutes. In general, such children are badly pampered and have no need to talk. Their mothers often say with pride that they always know what the child wants. Such children always want to be understood without having to talk, and they want to be paid attention to at all times. If such a child does not talk, and if the pampering person always performs the tasks demanded by the child, we can see how voluntary muteness arises. Also, we know that children develop and regulate all of their functions in accordance with their environment.

I know the case of a child born to a deaf-mute couple, who was himself perfectly normal: he spoke and understood normally. If he was hurt he would begin to cry, but without any sound. The tears would run down his cheeks, and his facial expression would be sad, but no one could hear him cry. He knew that it was useless to make any noise. Functions develop according to the environment. They can't develop any other way. You can conclude the so called psychology of drives in these considerations, because drives develop only in accordance with the environment. This boy was spared the necessity of talking; therefore his speech capacity did not develop in time.

"At present he talks in a somewhat nasal voice. His tonsils and adenoids were removed four years ago, and it is likely that more work will have to be done on his adenoids soon. He is a slightly Mongoloid type."

We are somewhat surprised to learn that he is a "Mongoloid type." There is reason to suspect that he may after all belong to the feeble-minded children. But I am not altogether sure that he should be classed as a Mongoloid type. Up to the present time no Mongoloid child has ever been found who was not feeble-minded. But it must not be forgotten that certain people resemble Mongols without being feeble-minded.

"The root of his nose is wide, his ears are prominent, and his lower lip protrudes. Examination of the nervous system did not reveal anything in particular, and his intelligence is normal. His right leg is stiff. The child likes gymnastics very much, and he has been able to get permission to take part in exercises, as far as his leg allows him to, although originally he was forbidden to do any gymnastics."

I have often noticed that children with defects of the arms or legs are especially zealous about gymnastics and sometimes become very excellent. This confirms once again a fundamental thesis of Individual Psychology; namely, that the best results are obtained by a special interest provoked by an organic inferiority. A few years ago a one-legged dancer was giving performances in our city.

You can easily see that in the little time allowed us, we cannot achieve everything that one might do with this child. Our work would be very much facilitated if someone were willing to put himself at the disposal of the mother and the child. We must try to make the child more independent and more courageous; and by means of supplementary lessons he must be brought up to the point where he is capable of going to regular school again. We must offer him a goal, and show him how to achieve significant results on the useful side of life. As soon as he begins to succeed, and in proportion as he does so, his bad habits will cease to have a reason for being. (Enuresis was his last refuge.) We must show him a better way. We must also gain the mother's support for if we make this proposal to the child while the mother is against us, the boy will have difficulties. We want to show the mother the actual structure of the child's personality, and try to influence her.

Dr. A. (to the mother): We are going to talk about your child. Would you say that he is one of the best students in his class?

The mother: I wouldn't say that.

Dr. A.: Is he one of the best students in the remedial school?

The mother: He is doing pretty well, except for arithmetic. Other children are better than he is. The teacher says that if he doesn't read too fast everything is all right. But he speeds up. . . .

Dr. A.: What would he like to become?

The mother: A carpenter.

Dr. A.: What does his father do?

The mother (proudly): He's a dental technician. The grandfather has a furniture store. My father said he wanted the boy to learn the trade so he would know all about furniture.

Dr. A.: So he wants him to be a carpenter. Does the boy have friends?

The mother: Oh, yes. Always children younger than he is.

Dr. A.: Does he like to make friends with other children?

The mother: He only wants to play with children younger than he is.

Dr. A.: Does he go to a play center?

The mother: He used to go to the Children's Friends. Once the children had a fight. The teacher pulled their ears and threw them against the wall.

Dr. A.: Does he tell the truth?

The mother: He tells stories sometimes, but he doesn't lie.

Dr. A.: Does he know how to handle money?

The mother: Yes, he does.

Dr. A.: Is he reliable?

The mother: Yes, he is very reliable. He is very helpful in the business, and he knows exactly what he is doing. He answers the phone, and does little jobs very well. But he is very childish.

Dr. A.: How does he feel at school?

The mother: He feels fine at school. He used to go to a private school. We thought it would be easier for him. But they didn't pay much attention to him and they did not pass him. A psychiatrist gave him an examination and said he was normal, and advised us to place him in the remedial school.

Dr. A.: What kind of children do they have at the remedial school?

The mother: Those children are horrible, but he doesn't let it bother him. They have very backward children there. If I knew for sure that he could eventually support himself. . . .

Dr. A.: You have never doubted it?

The mother: The teachers always consoled me that he would become a good businessman. He is interested in everything. He knows how to talk about a lot of things, and he gives the impression of being independent. But he is so childish!

Dr. A.: Does he often wet himself?

The mother: Yes. I went to see the teacher and asked how he was behaving at school. The only thing she complained about was that he talked in too loud a voice. He'll have to get rid of that habit. He wets himself also at school. The teacher said it must be weakness. *Recently it has gotten worse.*

Dr. A.: Has his situation at school deteriorated?

The mother: He is making progress. He used to have somebody help him with his assignments. Now he does them all by himself.

Dr. A.: Hasn't he been criticized? In arithmetic, for example?

The mother: In arithmetic the others are better than he is.

Dr. A.: It would be good if he could make progress in that subject, too. Would you like to send the boy to our children's center? (Dr. A. gives her the address.) Can he come by himself?

The mother: Yes, he knows how to take the streetcar. He goes to school by himself.

Dr. A.: At this children's center they will be able to convince him that he can succeed at everything, and he will get to the point where he can go to regular school.

The mother: At the "Children's Friends" he did some good work, too. He made a beautiful theatre. He has something that lots of children lack. As the teacher says, he is very conscientious.

Dr. A.: It would be better for the boy to go to regular school. What kind of child is the other boy?

The mother: He is a wonderful boy.

Dr. A.: How does he behave toward the younger one?

The mother: They like each other a lot. Now, things have changed: I am with my parents, and the older boy is with his paternal grandmother, so they don't see each other very often.

Dr. A.: Does he tease the younger one?

The mother: He worries about him a lot. He is afraid for him.

Dr. A.: He behaves like a father. We often see this trait in an older child who has won out.

The mother: The older boy has always developed well.

Dr. A.: He seems to be very popular.

The mother: The little one is even more popular. The older boy is proud.

Dr. A.: Haven't people teased the little one, or made fun of him, because he is going to the remedial school?

The mother: They don't tease him on account of the school. But they tease him. They make fun of him because of his foot—it's terrible!

Dr. A.: That will die down—and so will his wetting himself. I advise you to encourage the child, and not criticize him or scold him. Encourage him to do everything by himself.

The mother: My family is always irritating him and criticizing him and scolding him.

Dr. A.: Please give them my regards and tell them they will have to refrain from criticizing, scolding, and nagging him. We are going to try a new method for his improvement.

(The mother leaves, after having expressed her thanks.)

Dr. A.: *Is it very important to learn that he is always attacked at home.* I don't know whether you have seen the tapir at the zoo. This tapir has a peculiar habit. If anyone irritates or annoys him, he turns his back on them and urinates. It is sometimes very annoying for an innocent bystander.

Dr. A. (to the child): How are you doing at school?

The child: Good.

Dr. A.: You are a smart boy, and you could be a good student. I have the feeling that you are cowardly—that you lack self-confidence. You believe you can't do well in arithmetic, but that's nothing very hard. You can do it easily. I'll help you to become good at arithmetic. Then we can arrange things so that you go to another school. I would like to help you in that, too. We'll go at it skillfully. You'll enjoy it; and all of a sudden people will say, "There! He's making progress!" I would like to have you go to my children's center. The children play games there. You could do your assignments there, and you would be happy. I was very poor at arithmetic, too. Someone had to show me how to do it, and then I became the best in the class. What would the teacher say if you became the best in arithmetic?

The child: She would be happy.

Dr. A.: Do you want to please her?

The child: Yes.

Dr. A.: Come back soon. And don't be upset if some boy says something stupid to you; it just means that *he's* stupid. If someone criticizes you at home, you mustn't get angry right away and wet yourself. I want you to help me. Can I count on you?

(The child leaves.)

* **20** *

The Child with Brilliant Brothers and Sisters

I am continuing the series of explanations by which I want to show you how I proceed. I have before me a series of reports on cases involving problem children—reports that I have not looked at for a long time. I would like to explore these cases with you and give you a rough idea of the way these cases should be examined. I would like to show you how, on the basis of our experience, we should examine each point in order to find the overall picture, to see all of the symptoms in our overall context. You will be able to understand what we mean by "explore" and "interpret"—notions that many authors have discussed, but which I maintain they have not adequately understood. If one chances to read explanations of Individual Psychology, one finds that the authors believe they have understood this psychology simply by referring to the "striving for self-importance" or by employing such expressions as "the feeling of inferiority" or "the striving for power." It has never been forgotten that this notion was employed by Nietzsche. Everyone believes he understands Individual Psychology. We have recently witnessed the development of a school which calls itself characterological, and which practices characterology in the wildest fashion. You will constantly find them citing the authority of Nietzsche. We should not let ourselves be bluffed, because we are not obliged to attribute psychological subtlety to those who cite this name. If today someone cites the name of Nietzsche in vain, he is already suspect.

"The child in question has had many childhood diseases."

Before mentioning that a child who has had many childhood diseases has been pampered, I would like to emphasize that Individual Psychology's principal aim is to explore and interpret the way one individual behaves toward another, since we do not know any other form of human expression. We know only that he *must* relate with his fellow creatures; and we must ascertain how he does it. This rule gives us a way of measuring. When I tell you that a child has had a great many childhood diseases, we can see the picture of a social connectedness taking shape. How did this child relate to his surroundings?

"He had diphtheria, and was given injections."

If the report was written by the parents, we can say that they were strongly impressed by the importance of the injections and that they see them as something frightening. It is certainly not a trifle to have diphtheria and get injections. But from the manner in which this report was drawn up, we can see the relation of the parents to us. They want to give us the impression that the child has suffered a great deal.

"During convalescence the child developed nervous troubles: he shook his shoulders, rubbed his hands against his thighs, and talked with extreme rapidity."

One may consider these symptoms as nervous troubles. But the nervous complications familiar to doctors as an after-effect of diphtheria are different. They include paralysis of the soft palate, of certain muscular groups, and of cerebral areas. But none of these things is involved in the present case. We are inclined to think it is either a tic or a voluntary movement with a purpose. A purpose may also be at the back of a tic, but it is not as evident. When we hear that a child draws attention to himself by rubbing his hands against his thighs, we have a confirmation of our notion that it does not involve an organic affliction. This child's behavior is noticeable; and we must remember that similar symptoms appear at the beginning of dementia praecox.

But according to the report, these symptoms appeared when the child was so young that such a disease is out of the question. We must therefore look for something else, and introduce our principal theme: What effects does this behavior have on others? It is a mode of expression, even if not a pretty one. By shaking his shoulders and rubbing his thighs the child certainly attracted the attention of his parents and of others around him. We must suppose that there was something wrong in his relationship to his parents, since children do not usually behave in this manner. We know from our own experience (and everyone will agree) that this kind of behavior attracts attention. Having already established that the boy must have been pampered, we shall assume that in his subsequent efforts to maintain this state of pampering he has adopted these mannerisms. This is not the most courageous way of putting oneself at the center of attention. The child does not appear to be sure of himself; otherwise he would have resorted to more common devices. For example, he would have worked hard, behaved nicely, and given a friendly and pleasant impression. He would have made progress on the useful side of life. It seems to me that this idea did not occur to him, because he lacked self-confidence.

"This child talks very rapidly."

We remember that this is an attempt to attract the attention of others by means of a particular manner of speech. These are intensive strivings which develop when there is a strong feeling of inferiority. It would be excellent if we could establish right now the cause of this feeling of inferiority. It is our task to find this out and no objection can make it easier. We must understand why this child resorts to such intensive strivings. If the child has once been, psychologically in a favorable situation (he has had diseases and been given injections) he will not voluntarily leave this pleasant situation. But the fate of such children and the course of events make it inevitable that they must leave this situation. When this happens, they have the feeling that they have been dethroned. In their striving for significance, a feeling which animates everyone, it is only natural that they seek means of becoming once more the center of attention. At present, although this child has been cured, he is nevertheless seeking a means of recovering the tenderness which was showered on him during his illness. Whether this is the only reason why this child is trying so hard to regain his pleasant situation I cannot say at this point. There are perhaps other causes as well. We must not be confused by the fact that other children show the same symptoms without having had serious diseases, since in fact almost all children go through a phase of being pampered. If the parents do not direct the child's interest toward other things and other people, any child in his first two or three years will get used to being pampered. This is why it is necessary to seek for other causes which might have reinforced the feeling of inferiority.

"The doctor whom we had consulted on several occasions, said that this trouble would disappear when the boy reached puberty."

I think it might be well if we accepted nothing else from this statement but the fact that the child had not yet reached puberty. This explanation given by the doctor is no more accurate, generally speaking, than any of the fantastic and even ludicrous theories of certain psychologists on the significance of puberty. They believe that puberty is a frightful phase; that sexuality ruins children; and that the child undergoes a fundamental change at this time. Actually, only one thing happens: the child gains more freedom, more strength, and greater possibilities; and he seems to hear within himself a kind of challenge, calling upon him to behave as if he were no longer a child. He nearly always replies to this challenge with excesses. In our day there is a strong tendency to try to understand the how and the why of an individual on the basis of the development of his sexual glands. Soon, now, we shall no longer be permitted to doubt that the seat of our intelligence is in the sex glands. Whatever happens, it is interpreted with great facility: If there is deterioration, it is the fault of puberty; and if there is improvement, puberty is still the cause. At this point, the study of puberty is already more of a refuge for fools than a field for research.

"The boy's father also suffered from timidity when he was a child, but to a lesser extent."

Here we can read between the lines that the child also suffers from timidity. I do not know how timidity is understood by those characterologists who claim to derive from Nietzsche. If we apply our social yardstick to it, this term indicates an underestimation of one's own person; or, which means the same thing, an overestimation of others. In other words, the boy feels weak. This weakness is expressed in intensive strivings—or arrogance toward his family. We are not surprised to see that when this boy, with his feeling of inferiority, encounters superior forces in strangers, the true content of his mentality becomes clearly apparent. His timidity means "staying on the sidelines"—being reluctant to join in with others. On the basis of this movement you can see what is involved here: he is a child who believes himself capable of nothing. When we have come this far, we won't find any surprises in other respects. Everything should take place as we can anticipate it. We can tell how he will behave in the face of any given social problem; for example, the problem of friendship.

"The other children do not suffer from this timidity."

Thus there are other children in the family. When we hear that the other children are not so timid, we can assume that they do not have such a marked feeling of inferiority. This strong feeling of inferiority may derive from the fact that the boy was excessively pampered, and that he leaned on some person for too long—a situation which had to come to an end some time. Having learned that there are other children in the family, we are entitled to assume that this boy probably experienced a second tragedy. Perhaps he was the youngest child for a certain period. (I won't go so far as to say that he started out as an only child.) The youngest child is more the center of attention than the others. And if, later on, another child takes his place, we can understand that he has experienced a worsening of his entire situation. If we learn that there now exists a youngest child who is perhaps the favorite of the family, we shall understand why this boy strives to make himself conspicuous.

"The oldest boy is finishing his studies at the university."

If one member of a family goes through college and another does not, it always provokes a great rage in the "common man." And perhaps not without reason. The younger boy might well say: "Why didn't you make *me* into such an outstanding man?" We shall try to find out whether the above comment does not mean: "This boy couldn't go that far." If this is what he has been made to feel, we shall have the necessary information to establish, finally, why the boy feels so inferior.

"The youngest boy is especially gifted."

This comment lends strong support to our suppositions.

"Two years ago, at the age of fifteen, he died suddenly of meningitis."

Now we have some information on the age of our subject: he is more than seventeen years old. He is old enough so that the question of college has come up already. We have learned that the youngest child was especially gifted. Imagine, if you will, the situation this boy had to cope with if he wanted to be significant. The older boy is a college student; the younger one is gifted; and he is in the middle. We do not yet know anything about his aptitudes. All we know is that he employs cheap devices. It is clear that he did not demonstrate an ability qualifying him for college; otherwise he would not have done such things as shaking his shoulders and rubbing his thighs; he would not have been timid. This does not mean that timid persons are not qualified for college work. But in this report we find that the presentation has the aim of persuading us that the boy is backward and cannot be compared to the other two. His symptoms are actually very minor as far as his backwardness is concerned. But if we had the boy before us in person, we would find a hundred other indications.

"The boy did not do very good work at school."

I can keep my promises. We are not going to learn anything new about this boy, only things we might expect. Our experience permits us to add that the boy is not feeble-minded. Everything that happens is a result of his style of life, as we foresaw. There is obviously intelligence and reason in his behavior.

"He has had to repeat a year of school on two occasions."

This setback probably didn't do much to encourage him. There are children who, when they have to repeat a year of school, get down to work and become good students and make rapid progress. But in general we find that being left back does damage to the child in the long run. I believe one should reflect carefully before making a child repeat a year of school, and should ask oneself whether other means might not be employed.

"By special authorization he was allowed to stay in school until the age of sixteen, which permitted him to finish all three years of trade school."

The report has told us to what extent he was retarded compared to his older brother. I must add (as was to be expected): he is a second child. He tries in every way to secure for himself the right of seniority. (Cf. Jacob and Esau.) There is only one way for him to dethrone an older brother who is so capable: to come into closer contact with his parents to win them over to his side by means which are essentially useless. Thus, what we have explained, and what other authors have never been able to clarify becomes apparent: If the younger of two brothers succeeds in catching up with the older so that he cannot lose the hope of being equal to him, he will develop unhindered and will have his own particular characteristics. He will always be under pressure, he will be on the move constantly and he will always run. If this mode of action succeeds for him to the point where he is able always to keep his courage and his hope, his development is assured. If he does not succeed—if he loses hope—he becomes a "problem child." This is something we must watch. The second child has this character trait: he presses forward as if in a race. I have always established this except in cases where there was a complete breakdown. Can we find signs of such a race even in the present case? The boy speaks very rapidly! Here you can see the high-strung movement: he wants to get ahead of others by means of speech.

"When he finished school he became an apprentice pastry-cook."

Once again we see the wide gap. You only have to understand what it means to have a brother who is a college student while you are an apprentice pastry-cook. It is not an easy situation; and it requires a great magnanimity to remain calm in the face of being relegated to the "average." If we had only this consolation to offer him, it would be better if we gave up our work. He would be perfectly justified if he abandoned everything.

"According to the information furnished by his employer, he suffers terrible anxiety if he is faced with difficult problems."

You can see how he is weighed down by his feeling of inferiority and his discouragement; and the great distance which separates him from the social problem of work. This can be understood only by applying the social yardstick. If you believe that this has something to do with his glands, his endocrine secretions, there is nothing we can do except give him more injections.

"He begins to shake, and he has to be relieved of his work."

This means that he has built his entire social life on the idea that someone else should do the work for him. This is the style of life of a pampered child who doesn't want to do anything by himself and is always looking for someone to help him.

"He was however very gifted at arithmetic."

I don't know what the parents mean by this. But since we have been able to establish that the boy worked hard at school, we can assume that he is competent in arithmetic on the level required in school.

"He could be entrusted with large sums of money. He has never lost anything, and has never done anything to invite criticism."

This means that he has never stolen, cheated, or lost anything. But he lacks the confidence to do anything on his own. He lives like a parasite. This, it must be admitted, is a harsh criticism. But his way of life is nothing but a tragic error. Because in this way he can never establish social relations.

"He is a particularly kind-hearted boy."

Some Freudians would probably object here and point out: His unconscious is no doubt full of hate for those around him—a resentment which could be denied in the case of discouragement—it would be plain that it came from his unconscious (Oedipus complex) and that there was no possibility of helping him. In this case he would be a boy possessed by a death wish and criminal inclinations. But we think he is probably a docile boy, certainly a good child, who would have liked to make contact with others. By this timidity—by the demonstration of his weakness—he tried to force kind behavior of others to him. You have heard that he shook so much he had to be relieved of his work. We believe that good naturedness is his dominant character trait, in both his conscious and his unconscious.

"He is very good at mental arithmetic, and he memorizes very rapidly."

He is well trained, and it is likely that throughout his life he would have been a good student; but he never got beyond that stage. When he had to face life itself, he showed that he was not prepared for it.

"He has a good ear for music, and he is interested in literature. His favorite pastime is to visit museums."

When his parents say he is interested in literature, they mean that he likes to read. However, this is suspect, because reading enables him to escape the real problems of life.

"He can understand lectures correctly, and he can summarize them perfectly."

This last comment gives us something to think about. He likes to read, he likes to visit museums, and we hear that he goes to lectures which he can repeat correctly. All this means that he is trying to emulate his brother, who, he knows, reads a lot and goes to lectures. As you can see, he does not allow himself to give in, and he strives to raise himself up even though he is an apprentice pastry-cook. This is the point where we would try to raise him to a higher level. We could understand that his anxious trembling is connected with his striving to find an occupation in another area. He is not satisfied with his job as pastry-cook. He has only one desire: to have someone else do that job for him. He prefers intellectual work. At the museum he does not tremble; he shows he is capable. It seems that this path remains blocked for him, since no one understands him, and also perhaps because he has had to repeat a year of school on two different occasions.

"He talks with frightful rapidity."

We have already touched upon this point: he wants to be first.

"His glance is furtive and lowered."

It is the mode of expression of the eyes which reveals timidity—the reluctance to establish contact with other eyes. Our sensory organs have social functions, too—even though it may *shock* other psychologists! They seek contact, like the organs of speech. Language represents an attempt to establish contact with others. In his "eye language" the boy expresses the feeling of his weakness, just as in his speech he shows his weakness by his rapid talking. He fears that he will be defeated if he does not talk so fast.

"He has no interest in sports."

Obviously.

"He was exempted from gymnastics while he was in school because of gland trouble in the region of the groin."

Here we see, once again, a reflection of his being pampered. That a person should be exempted permanently from gymnastic exercises because of gland trouble strikes me as exaggerated. This gland trouble was probably due to a little lesion between the toes. People usually get over these things very quickly.

"When he took the compulsory medical examination at the apprentices' home, the doctors diagnosed a nervous disease, and the boy was supposed to take a special course of treatment. But the plan didn't work out because the employer couldn't do without him, owing to a lack of personnel and a temporary increase in business."

We must therefore assume that he made himself useful in spite of everything.

"Recently the boy passed his apprentice's examination brilliantly. But his parents are very apprehensive about the future. They are convinced that the boy cannot cope with the demands of his trade and the work that it requires."

Despite the fact that he passed the apprentice's examination with honors. There are certainly not many parents who would have apprehensions in such a case. This boy seems always to have been the object of his parents' worries. It is probably this very attitude which contributed to the boy's discouragement. They never believed he was capable of anything; they were always apprehensive about his future, something which was not justified. The child should have been encouraged. The best way to do this would be to enlighten the boy as to his errors. I don't know whether one can call that a theory, since it is not to be classed with other psychological theories. We would not be disturbed if a layman working with this boy, arrived at the same conclusion. But we should not be reproached for coming to these conclusions more quickly with our methods of investigation. Apparently the occupation with psychology and philosophy has made these people shortsighted for real life. This is very regrettable, but we are not to blame for it. One post-script on how immensely sexuality is overestimated in our time.

"It should be noted that not the slightest sexual urge has been observed in this boy."

He is seventeen or eighteen years old. It might be countered that the parents may know nothing about him in this regard. But if we are correct, we shall be able to demonstrate that the parents made an accurate observation. If this boy were in fact courageous in his social relationships (and sexual strivings also represent a social relationship) we would be faced with a contradiction that we could not explain. But the organization of his drives shows exactly the same modifications as are shown by the rest of his life. It may be that he inherited a drive strong beyond imagining. Perhaps since his birth he has had the most perverse drives, the drives of an extraordinarily potent individual, or—on the contrary—the most feeble drives. But this cluster of drives will nonetheless conform to this boy's dominant goal; i.e., to keep himself at a distance and escape the solution of his problems; to make others do his work for him.

We can venture a look into the future. We must agree with the parents that there will be difficulties if the boy does not change his style of life. He will show a greater distance in all areas. We hear nothing of friends. The same is true of occupation and love. We can guess his movements, and the distance which he will manage to keep from all these problems. When he finds a crutch, when he becomes a student, he will not make himself conspicuous. But when he has to behave like a man, it will become evident that he has not taken seriously his own role as a man.

I would like to add one word about education. Although it may be redundant. The method of education derives automatically from the exploration of the child's style of life and the errors we have found there. The boy must be encouraged. The only way to do this is to draw his attention to the correct point. He must realize that he is not making progress in life because he was very pampered. He must realize himself that he approaches everything with the question: What will this bring me? That he is seeking warmth and appreciation, and help from others. It is not so very difficult to make a person understand this. If one goes at it with the proper psychological tact and grasps the problem with the artist's intuition, one will succeed.

We must abandon the idea that he has less talent than his brother. Someone must explain to him that he can succeed in everything, provided he trains himself adequately. It is essential to clear a path for him. The mother and father must not persist in saying, "You will never succeed at anything." It would be good if the boy believed none of this, but he experienced a few setbacks because he approached life from the wrong side and with the unfortunate idea that someone else should do everything for him. We must make him understand all this, and enlighten him on the fact that he has not yet reached the limits of his potentialities. We must tell him: 'You are interested in lectures and you follow them, because you are prepared for them and because you were a good student." He has the advantage of having exercised his brain in this direction. He can be encouraged to the point where he will be able to "beat" his brother. This is the banner under which we must advance: He who gets over difficulties will win out!

Pedagogical tact and artistic comprehenison of problems are both social functions. Pedagogical tact signifies the attitude of one man toward another, which is determined by a desire to raise the level of the others' feeling in a kind manner. How can we explain this attitude? Briefly, one has to reproduce the same feeling in oneself, one has to establish contact with the other person. One must see with the other person's eyes, hear with his ears, and feel with his heart: one must identify with him. This is a totally different process than that which corresponds to Freudian theory. It is more of a process which in psychology is called "empathy." It can be learned only in society, when the relationship of the "I" to the "you" has been built up in a useful fashion, when one has adopted the idea of being a "fellow being." Training is not accomplished in a vacuum but in the social relationships between the self and others. One must experience all forms of social relationships: friendship, interest in others. We must strive to become what we ask that our children become—neither more nor less.

When I take up the artistic aspect of our work, I am walking on a volcano, since this is the idea of all psychological parasites, who pretend to be deeply offended when we advance the idea. They claim to be the only ones who regard this art so highly as art while "we don't understand anything about it." I have always found that when I have approached an artist with our way of understanding things, it has given him greater dignity. When we observe artists we do not consider them incomprehensible, as someone who can never be understood. Rather, we endow them with the greatest honor: that of being human beings, fellow men, and leaders of humanity. It is they who have taught us how to see, think, and feel. We are indebted to them for mankind's greatest boons. If, once again, we apply the social yard stick, we shall see that the artist performs a social function in the largest sense. There was a time when this was generally realized; but today it has been forgotten. I am thinking of the note of introduction sent by Lessing to Schiller on the occasion of the opening of the Hamburg theatre: "The theatre considered as a moral institution." The artist should strive only to enrich humanity, to open up new avenues for a better understanding and more profound feeling. And here once again we stand on firm ground—on the very foundation of Individual Psychology.

* 21 *

How I Talk to Parents

I believe it is important to speak, in the right way, to the parents. How that is to be done is difficult to put into words. It would be a good idea for all counselors to discuss this question among themselves from time to time. The first thing is to win the confidence of the parents. One must not antagonize them. When parents come to us for consultation, it is because they feel responsible. They expect to be criticized. Above all, one must relieve them of this fear. Usually I tell parents, "It seems to me that you are on the right track," even when I am convinced of the contrary. If I want to accomplish something, I must choose an appropriate method. I noticed, in an old biography of Benjamin Franklin, that he went about things in this same way. He dispensed with all dogmatic lecturing.

In regard to details, I have noticed that it is well not to question the mothers too much. In consultations involving students we have the assistance of the teacher. Teachers have understood the importance of these guidance centers. We psychologists are in a relatively favorable position. The teacher and the mother live with the child during the rest of the day. They have the heaviest burden. It is most important to grasp the essential point of the case; but it is just as important not to burden the mother immediately with what one has learned. This we must keep to ourselves, and only allude to it on occasion. It is essential to acquire this aptitude and to proceed in this fashion.

The critical sense of psychologists and teachers is deeply rooted. I recommend the use of expressions like "perhaps" or "I think that would work very well." We are not in a position to treat the parents too. We can only give them some pointers. It is impossible to modify a deeply-rooted system with a few words. Moreover, it is superfluous when we can gain the confidence of the children and show them that they should not take a tragic view of their difficulties—that it is more important to be courageous. A counselor is in a position to encourage, in a half-hour, a child who is near a breakdown, because we are in a privileged position: We are dealing with children who have been criticized. Suddenly they find themselves in a new atmosphere where they may realize that they are not considered to be hopelessly lost. It would be good if we could be in longer contact with these children—if we had a sufficient number of counselors. Unfortunately we cannot publish statistics; but the teachers report encouraging results.

One must win over the parents immediately. Each counselor can develop this method to a very high degree. We tend *a priori* toward gentleness, and are pledged to it. Some counselors have achieved a genuine mastery in the matter of gentle treatment. This is necessary when one is discussing such faults as rage. But we must never forget that this is only the form, and that we must clarify the essence, that we must elucidate the style of life. This is the great advantage which distinguishes us from others. We have to do this in full awareness and as a matter of course. It is not our purpose to bribe the children so that they will give up their erroneous ways. Rather, we aim at the central problem: Their hopelessness, the error that they have lost hope. This is the core of the problem; the rest is only preparatory.

Thus, we must start out by winning the child. But those who believe that this will bring about a cure, are gravely mistaken. But if a cure is effected it is an accident not an achievement. These are situations where the child understands something that the counselor has yet failed to grasp. It is not enough to be a friend of the human race and a kindly counselor. Everybody tries to do that. They make life pleasant for the children, praise them constantly, and imagine that they will get results by the charm of their personality.

It is pointless to dwell upon the controversy as to whether one should employ kindness or severity. Access to the human soul is gained only through modesty. It is an art to win someone over, to awaken certain feelings in him, to induce him to listen, and understand what is said to him—and this art is indispensable when working with children. We hear people say, "At the child-guidance center the child is often nice, but at home he is worse than the devil." If the child has understood, it marks the first step toward a more amiable relationship. One cannot constantly maintain a child in favorable circumstances. One cannot make his faults disappear by pampering him. Rather, he must be made to understand what has been wrong with his development; and in this area we are guided by the system of Individual Psychology. Sometimes it only requires ten minutes for a counselor to be completely clear about a case. The art consists in making someone else understand this. There are people who have a great deal of knowledge but cannot communicate it. Those who have good contact with people will have an easier task, since in their daily dealings with people they have learned how to make themselves understood. This is the primary task of the counselor in Individual Psychology.

* 22 *

The Task of the Kindergarten

There is certainly no need to call your attention to the very great importance of a child's training when he is of school age. The new psychology that I represent—Individual Psychology—has stressed that the time of a child's entry into school is the most important time in his life. It is a fact that after the fourth and fifth years a child's style of life is already so well defined that external influences can no longer change it. It was formerly believed that a child's behavior varied in accordance with situations and at different ages. A green fruit differs in appearance from a ripe fruit. However, an expert can tell what it will become. I would like to stress that this unripe fruit is more than an unfolding entity. It represents something alive, *striving*, with a psychic movement which tends toward an ideal form, and which will face the tasks of life from this fixed vantage point, and will have to come to terms with them. Every one of a child's strivings is already automatic, in these early years. These movements are no longer conscious, thought through in every instance. But, they are the answers to all problems of existence, determined by the style of life. Children can be differentiated by their psychic behavior. The true expert will rarely make a mistake once he has established that a child is timid or reserved, or that when faced with a task he approaches it gingerly or keeps as far away from it as possible; hesitates, or tries to escape. These are only small details, but we can gain much information from them. We cannot consider a small child separate and apart from human society. The foundations of individuality and personality are laid in the first four or five years. When something goes wrong then, it cannot be changed by external measures.

Our inner life is nothing but forms of relationships. It is very interesting, in physiology and biology, to search for individual parts, e.g., what are drives and instincts. But it has no psychology. Here belong only relationships. For example, if a child is not asked, we will hardly obtain an indicative answer. We will not find out how he answers until we ask him; until we confront him with a task. In a pleasant situation, you will not betray the devil hidden in you. But once you are faced with a difficulty, you will reveal yourself. A child's state of mind appears only when there is such a confrontation. For us, "soul" and "psyche" mean social relationship and social striving. We are going to see where this social relationship comes from, and why it is so varied.

Everything that we can observe in a child, has had its potentiality since his birth. We cannot examine a child's capacities for the future, any more than we can know how far it will be possible for us to develop them. By employing a correct method, one can develop prodigiously from a small potentiality. For example, Helen Keller, deaf and blind, became an eminent personality. We have often seen that slight capabilities of a child developed to considerable proportions because a correct method had been found. The development of a child's faculties is much more a result of training than of the capacities he possesses. To establish a parallel: One man has a great fortune, but he does not know what to do with it, he squanders everything and finds himself caught short. Another man, who has but few resources, gets along very well.

The job of the kindergarten teacher is to clear the path and open the way so that the style of life in the first four or five years becomes such that it enables the child to solve all the tasks in life. There should be an ideal—not one to be attained, but to show the way. Education with a view to developing sociable human beings is not simply a hollow idea. One must make the child understand that a lack of sociability is the worst error that he can commit in his life.

How was the first relationship established? It is in the person of his mother that the child has his first experience with a fellow human being. And through the mother the child becomes interested in the others. This first experience is very important for the child. And the manner in which he experiences his mother is even more important.

Kindergarten teachers are in the place of the mother. They have to fulfill the functions of the mother. They must correct the errors made by the mother. They must guide the children in order to enable them to establish relations with others. This relation between "I" and "you" plays a major role in all of the individual's important faculties. Speech, for example, is such a relationship. The voice is the link between one human being and another. If this link is not completely developed, speech will not develop well. All children whose speech has not developed well (and who do not have organic defects) are children who have not been adequately prepared for the relationship between the "I" and the "you" relationship. You can draw conclusions about a man from the poverty or richness of his language, since he can exert himself and acquire a rich vocabulary only in a social milieu where he contracts relationships and accepts them.

Intelligence is not a private affair. To understand means to think, judge, conclude, etc., in such a fashion as I assume every reasonable man will think and draw just such conclusions. Intelligence has general validity. It cannot be fashioned according to a personal point of view.

You will notice that problem children have private ideas which we do not consider reasonable. They do not correspond to common sense. The same holds true for beauty and ugliness. What we call beautiful also has general validity.

The mother's first function is to awaken a sense of social feeling in the child by giving him the impression of a fellow human being. You will find many children who never got this impression and who do not know that there are fellow human beings. This applies especially to orphans and illegitimate children—but there are no rules, and among such children you will perhaps find some who do have social feelings. These children grow up without experiencing fellowship. This lack of social feelings is also found in ugly children, unwanted children, and cripples. One should realize the effect produced on them: always rejected without ever hearing a kind word. They grow up as if they were in an enemy country.

It is the teacher's task to give them the impression of a true fellow creature. This is a beautiful mission. If you adopt this point of view, you will not make many errors.

The mother's role involves another important function. During the first years of her child's life she must guide his interest towards others. She must not arrest it and fix it on herself. For example, pampered children are interested only in their mothers or the person who pampers them, but not in others. They want to exclude everybody else. When you see this tendency you can be sure that you are dealing with a pampered child who demands that everything be made easy for him, and that someone else always do something for him.

Teachers must guide the awakening social feeling further, and advise the mother that she should also direct this interest toward the father, so that together they can fix the child's style of life. Also, one must prepare the child for the possible arrival of younger brothers or sisters. This is a point that is often neglected and which has a strong influence on the child's style of life.

Kindergarten is an extension of the family. It must accomplish and correct those things which have not been done in the family, owing to poor understanding or old traditions. The teachers get the children already not as a blank page. At this age they already possess an individuality which will in no way be changed by experiences. Thanks to their intellectual superiority, the teachers may succeed in preventing children from certain acts. They may hide things, keep secrets, etc. But the style of life will still reappear. If you want to correct and eliminate a child's faults, you must perform the two functions of the mother. The child will notice his own faults, and he can correct them himself. Certain children whose attention has been drawn to their faults, deprecate everything in accordance with their style of life, and draw conclusions in their own way—which is not that of common sense nor of reason. A pampered child will try either to become the center of attention or eventually will run away. Such a child will be unable to overcome difficulties when he meets them. And if you take something away from him, he will always conclude: "I'm not where I belong. I was better off near Mamma." Such children always betray their feeling of being uncomfortable and show that they do not feel at home. If you perform the mother's two functions in her stead, and establish social contact, you will see remarkable results. The child will accept difficulties without anxiety and will try to overcome them in a useful manner. You will find that the child has courage. Courage is a social function. Only someone who considers himself a part of the whole can be courageous. Optimism, activity, courage, and fellowship depend on how one gives the child, early enough an education within the framework of society. The development of the individual can be guaranteed only if his social feeling is sufficiently large. If I take an interest in the well-being of others, my individuality is assured, and I can make myself useful to others. If I think only of myself, I am absolutely unfit to solve the problems of this life.

I would like to draw your attention to something obvious which is however still not properly understood. For every solution of a problem a developed social feeling is necessary. A child's social feeling is already manifested in the way he reacts to the birth of a second brother or sister. The task of the kindergarten teacher is a social one. School, friendship, love, marriage, political position, and artistic accomplishments are all social tasks. For us, art and science represent accomplishments useful to society. If a person has no social feeling, he is ignorant of the path he should take. This is why we should develop the social feeling of the children. How does it happen that so many children, even so many adults, have a lack of the social feeling? Individual Psychology has uncovered the obstacles to the correct development of social feeling.

We have been able to establish that hated and pampered children are overburdened. This is easy to understand in the case of hated children. But what about the pampered ones? Our entire social life is aimed at preventing the pampering of those who as children have been so much pampered in their early years. Little by little the mother herself ceases to be so indulgent, and finds the child's demands exaggerated. The child experiences continual rejections, but at the same time he is trying to maintain his initial pleasant position. So he begins to grow up in a hostile atmosphere. The first reaction of such a child is to be more interested in himself than in others.

For example, it is easy to observe that in a kindergarten this reaction can sometimes develop into panic. These children vomit, refuse to eat, and show evident symptoms of an inner tension bordering upon illness. They feel that their position is threatened. They are egoists. This is not a healthy condition. When the time comes for them to face a social problem they will not have the necessary training to enable them to acquire friends and to establish a rapport with the teacher. They cannot concentrate because they are always afraid. If you punish a child of this kind he will feel even more oppressed and threatened. If these children are arrogant it is because they feel small and weak. They behave as if they were standing on tip-toe in order to appear bigger than they actually are.

There is a third type of child who for the most part is incapable of developing any interest in others. These are children who were born weak, sickly, or with organic deficiencies. They consider their weakness, their illness a great burden, and are just as oppressed by this as the other types. They try to find an easier situation. Because of their organic inferiority they have little or no courage, and no confidence in themselves. They are very much rapt up in their deficiencies. Some of them try to overcome their weakness, whereas others fall into despair. For example, children with weak vision are for the most part better trained to perceive visible things than those with good vision. They are particularly interested in a better realization of visual things in one way or another: they are more aware of color, shadow, and perspectives. Their visual weakness gives rise to a great strength. These facts apply with equal force to other organic inferiorities: in hearing, respiration, the digestive apparatus, etc.

Thus, children entering kindergarten have a varied degree of courage. In certain cases each thought and each feeling becomes an indication enabling one to understand what is taking place in the soul of the child. It is very important to ascertain whether a child is feeble-minded. In the case of idiocy or imbecility the development cannot attain a normal degree. These children must be educated in a very different manner. They will never attain the level of normal children. It is very difficult to determine whether a child is feeble-minded. It can be decided only on the basis of collaboration among teacher, psychologist, and doctor. In certain cases one suspects feeble-mindedness. The less severe cases require a great deal of experience on the doctor's part. Many body anomalies do not affect the intelligence in any way. The fact that a child is hydrocephalic or microcephalic is not sufficient basis for diagnosing feeble-mindedness. One must first establish whether a child has suffered because of errors in his upbringing. Perhaps tests should be tried first of all. Feeble-minded children have no definite style of life. One cannot predict the behavior of a feeble-minded child in the face of a given task unless he has been trained in this matter. He cannot strive for a coherent style of life, because he lacks the unity of human psychic life. One must first of all establish whether a child is feeble-minded, since the action to be taken varies radically with the case. The child's psychic life should be explored thoroughly. It must be understood. Then the ways of education will become immediately apparent.

Kindergarten teachers also get left-handed children, without being aware of this fact. These children are clumsy, and have difficulty in writing and reading. Examine them and see whether they are left-handed. (Parents' statements are of no importance.) Such a child becomes discouraged easily. He realizes the weakness of his right hand, and he feels like a rejected child. A child also becomes discouraged easily if others make fun of him and are always teasing him. He loses his courage and becomes timid. One should realize also that an excessively severe upbringing causes great damage. It is impossible for this kind of weak and helpless human being to make contact with others if he has lost all courage. You will also encounter children whose mother has always spoken for them. One sees that the mother has spared him any effort, so that he has become completely dependent. Perhaps he has a speech defect, or cannot concentrate because his thinking powers are not correctly developed. Other children will stop talking in the middle of a sentence. These are children whose mothers are always interrupting them without giving them time to get a word out. They will always bear the mark of this. You must understand all these forms of expression in order to determine a child's degree of courage and optimism.

Rivalry between siblings plays a very important role. It is necessary to know the respective position of birth of each child. The fact should not be overlooked that a child is the oldest, a second child or the youngest, an only child, or the only girl amongst boys, the only boy among girls, etc.

We can compare children to shrubs in a thicket: they are all seeking the light.

The situation of an oldest child is totally different from that of a second child. He has been the only child for a certain period; then suddenly his *Lebensraum* is reduced by the birth of another child. For him this is a tragedy. Later on, such children behave as if they were afraid that someone else would surpass them. They will always be on the lookout to see whether someone else is preferred to them. They will always strive to be in the foreground.

The second child has never been alone; he has never been the center of attention. His situation is better: he has a "Pathmaker" who makes things easier for him in many respects. As though in a competition, he behaves as if he were trying to overtake the one who precedes him—provided nothing prevents him from doing so.

The youngest child grows up in quite a different situation. No one follows him, but several precede him. He has certainly the greatest advantage. He shows his strivings openly, and he wants above all to prove that he is the first. This striving is rewarded, because such a child is especially well-armed in his struggle against difficulties.

He who overcomes wins! Hence we must try to give children the "material" which will enable them to overcome. We must give them courage: this is the most important factor of education. The most dangerous thing is if a child loses hope. There are many difficult situations in the life of a child, but it must never lose hope.

In conclusion, let me add that one should never fight with children, for the simple reason that they are always the stronger ones. They do not take any responsibility. And he who assumes responsibility is never the stronger one.

Practice will be our real task. No education takes place in a vacuum. You will have to struggle with the difficulties which result from different interpretations of scientific research. We welcome comparison. We are tolerant. You should study other theories and points of view. Compare everything carefully, and don't blindly believe any "authority"—not even me!